Applied Psychology for Social Workers

Second Edition

Paula Nicolson
and
Rowan Bayne

palgrave

First edition 1984
Reprinted twice
Second edition 1990

Published by
PALGRAVE
Houndmills, Basingstoke, Hampshire RG21 6XS and
175 Fifth Avenue, New York, N. Y. 10010
Companies and representatives throughout the world

PALGRAVE is the new global academic imprint of
St. Martin's Press LLC Scholarly and Reference Division and
Palgrave Publishers Ltd (formerly Macmillan Press Ltd).

ISBN 0–333–49501–2 hardcover
ISBN 0–333–49502–0 paperback

This book is printed on paper suitable for recycling and made from fully managed and sustained forest sources.

A catalogue record for this book is available from the British Library.

10   9   8
04   03   02

Printed in Hong Kong

For Hilary Wild

Contents

List of Figures

Acknowledgements

Paula Nicolson would like to thank the students at Hillcroft College and those in the Department of Sociology at the Polytechnic of East London, who inspired many of the thoughts that first gave rise to this book. Since then there have been many positive changes in the discipline of psychology which have encouraged me to become more involved with psychology itself. My renewed enthusiasm comes from my contact with students and colleagues in the Department of Psychology at PEL and particularly my friends in the Psychology of Women section of the BPS.

Derry and Kate Nicolson and Jo Campling also deserve affectionate mention for their encouragement.

Polytechnic of East London   PAULA NICOLSON

Rowan Bayne would like to thank Linda Robinson, and the many people who introduced me to different aspects of interviewing and counselling, especially Clive Fletcher (as selection interviewer), Edgar Anstey (research on selection interviewing), Francesca Inskipp (basic counselling skills), Peter Cook (Egan) and Chris Lewis (selection interviewer training). I feel very warm and happy as I remember the difference they made. Ian Horton, Vicki Smith and Jan Woodley made helpful comments on drafts of Chapters 3 and 5, and Susamma Pius word-processed with patience and skill.

Polytechnic of East London   ROWAN BAYNE

Introduction

Since the first edition of this book, there have been several changes in the disciplines of social work and psychology. Social work has incorporated much of what we call psychology, as distinct from psychoanalysis, into its own theory and practice. Paradoxically, this has meant that psychology teaching on social work courses continues to be seen as an additional (if not 'optional') extra, and social workers now embrace such areas as 'behavioural social work' and 'cognitive therapy' as their own. As psychologists we are left with mixed feelings. On the one hand it is a positive achievement that mainstream academic psychology should contest the supremacy of psychoanalysis, which so heavily engulfed social work theory and practice in the 1950s and 1960s. On the other hand, the more vigorously social work theory claims psychological approaches for its own, the less significance the subject of psychology has for social workers.

This is not something that should only concern boundary jealous psychologists. We believe that it is the co-existence and cross-fertilisation of distinct disciplines that are to their mutual advantage, and argued this strongly in the first edition for both psychology and social work.

Psychology and social work have their individual strengths and different emphases. The study of psychology provides a framework for explanation of human behaviour and a particular set of professional practices. Social work is a practice-based profession which is informed by various disciplines – including psychology.

In this revised edition, we want to identify the progress which has been achieved over the last six years, and show how initiatives within the profession of psychology and those derived from psychological research will benefit social work educators, field work supervisors, students and practitioners.

We have therefore attempted two main tasks. Firstly to provide an overview of the *knowledge* that psychology has to offer to social work practice, and secondly, in Chapter 3 in particular, to provide a practical guide to interviewing and counselling, thus applying *skills which have been studied in psychology.*

Rowan Bayne has re-written Chapters 3 and 5 to include the most recent developments in these areas. There are new sections in Chapter 5 on psychological type, and in Chapter 3 on counselling and assertiveness. These two chapters (and to a lesser extent Chapter 4) are different in tone from the rest of the book. This partly reflects the distinct aim of these chapters which we intend to be guides to self-development of the particular skills, through complementing other forms of training rather than replacing them.

Paula Nicolson has substantially revised Chapters 1, 2, 6 and 9, and made minor revisions to Chapters 4, 7 and 8. The changes in the first two chapters reflect those in both disciplines, covering the way in which ideas from mainstream psychology now compete with psychoanalytic ones for a central place within social work theory, and the ways in which psychological research has been applied to social work problems. Chapter 6 has focussed upon the life course, particularly suggesting 'loss and change' as a continuing theme. It also takes account of research initiatives in the area of the psychology of women. Chapter 9 takes a fresh look at the future of psychology and social work in the light of preceding chapters.

1

What is Psychology?

Introduction

Psychology itself is not a unified discipline, but brings together a number of approaches and theoretical orientations to the study of the *individual*. Its origins as an academic subject area – the science of mind and behaviour – go back around one hundred years. In its brief history there have been a number of crises or turning points, and although western academic psychology today is well established, there are several areas of contention which provide stimulus to the growth of the discipline.

Psychology also informs the theory and practice of other disciplines from research in neurophysiology to applications of psychiatry, and has a variety of specific contributions to make towards social work theory and practice.

In the course of every social work encounter with every client a range of implicit and explicit uses of psychological knowledge may be introduced. Consider the following example. A man has called the Local Authority Social Services Department two weeks after his wife's admission to a psychiatric hospital. He is caring for their three children under school age, with the help of a child minder, with financial assistance and help from a series of relatives and friends. He feels depressed, anxious and no longer confident to cope with what he sees as an indefinite period of lone fatherhood. The social worker needs to assess this man's current predicament and make joint plans. So what exactly can psychology contribute here?

First, there is the immediate situation of trying to interview the man to make sense of the situation, to find out

1

all the relevant details from practical to emotional ones. This is not an easy task, especially when someone quite clearly is worried, and the social worker is very busy. Relaxation techniques (see Chapter 3) are helpful for the interviewer, along with the ability to create an atmosphere of calm so that both participants feel able to explore the situation together. This is in part created by making it clear to the client that what he says is being listened to and understood. The interviewer will also need to attend to his non-verbal cues (e.g. nailbiting, playing with hair, eye contact and so on), and non-verbal cues that she herself might be giving.

Secondly, psychology can help the social worker understand and evaluate the biographical material provided by the client. This includes assessing the immediate significance of the way the client is feeling, his previous and current relationship with his children and the friends who are helping, and of course his feelings and behaviour towards his wife and how this is and will continue to affect the family.

Thirdly, knowledge of the psychological strains and benefits of community versus institutional care and family life underpin assessment of the present situation and plans for change.

Finally the social worker her/himself will have a perception of the interview and the information gained from it, that is not an 'objective' reality, but the result of a 'filtering' through various psychological processes connected with the individual social worker's own circumstances. On each of these levels psychology has a contribution to make which helps social workers in their practice. There is no pro-forma for action – applying psychological knowledge relies on experience, but this cannot come about without a basic understanding of psychology itself, and what it has to offer.

In the following chapters we intend to demonstrate that psychological knowledge complements intuition in making judgements during face-to-face encounters with clients and in long-term assessments of services. It is also valuable in the self-assessment and personal growth of the practitioner, and enables an understanding of the organisations with which social workers are involved.

It is vital that links between psychology and social work practice be made explicit, so that social workers might develop appropriate skills in an informed and organised way, to the advantage of their clients and their profession.

What is psychology?

Psychology is an academic and an applied professional discipline. The term 'psychology' is also applied to common sense or intuitive understanding of 'how people tick' and many believe 'we are all natural psychologists' (see Howe, 1987, p. 107). Clearly this statement contains some truth, as none of us could survive if we did not employ some intuitive understanding of others. There is, however, a world of difference between a socially competent human being, the 'friend' with concern for others, and the professional social worker who is required to make judgements about a client's behaviour based on previous knowledge of that person and a valid prediction of how she will cope in the future.

Social workers have to do more than 'get along' with other people – they seek to make objective assessments and take decisions that radically affect the course of people's lives. For that they need access to a scientific discipline – psychology.

Academic psychology

Academic psychology (the substance of research and teaching) embraces a number of different approaches, although broadly speaking the focus of attention is upon the individual. Social psychology is to some extent an exception to this rule, although still retains a substantial focus on the interaction between individuals. Academic psychology has a separate history from psychoanalysis with its origins in psychiatry, although increasingly psychoanalytic material is being introduced (albeit in a tentative way) into under-graduate and post-graduate courses.

Although there are various approaches within academic psychology, it is overall a *scientific* discipline. This means that its theory and practice are based upon *empirical* evidence derived from observations rather than on opinions, beliefs, prejudice or argument. These observations are not casual ones, but reliable and repeatable according to a fairly strict set of rules. Measurement is crucial, and the data (generated by observations) have to be compiled in a systematic way. There are inevitable problems for a discipline which requires the assessment of people by other people, and in order to meet the constraints imposed by the scientific method, the focus of energies has been upon the study and analysis of *behaviour*, often using the *experimental* method. Although this has ensured the rigour which science demands, it has also meant that the scope of the discipline has been limited in certain ways, at the expense of studying emotions and feelings in everyday situations. The scope and potential of academic psychology are constantly developing, which is the main reason for revising this book. It is important for social workers to understand the ground rules of this particular discipline, so that *they* can initiate relevant research projects to shed light onto problems faced in practice.

Before specifying the content of the various approaches, we shall put them into an historical context.

Psychoanalysis and behaviourism emerged in the late nineteenth century, but developed in very different ways. Psychoanalysis was the work of Sigmund Freud in Vienna, a neurologist whose early work with hysterics led him to explore psychological techniques which probed the unconscious. These included 'free association' and the analysis of fantasies and dreams. Behavioural psychology concentrated on 'objectivity', observation and measurement and had its origins in animal psychology.

Cognitive-developmental psychology is an offshoot of cognitive psychology, itself developed as a reaction to behaviourism which ignored 'what goes on inside the heads' of human beings. Cognitive-developmental psychology attempts to explore the maturational changes in mental structures as well as the changes in capacities which occur as the infant becomes the child and then the adult.

Social psychology has origins in sociology as well as psychology, with Comte in France and Cooley in America (at the turn of the century) both making reference to 'social psychology'. The 1930s and 1940s were another period of growth with studies of industrial management and army leadership inspiring researchers.

Humanistic psychology is rooted in the optimism of the 1960s and the work of Abraham Maslow, George Kelly and Carl Rogers. Rogers' work in particular was derived from his therapeutic work and, like Freud, he developed a theory of personality and human development based on his clinical experience. Unlike psychoanalysis however, humanistic psychology emphasises the positive nature of human beings and their efforts towards growth and self-actualisation or self-fulfilment.

Psychoanalytic psychology

This approach is based on the work of Sigmund Freud, but has also been developed by others such as Erikson, Melanie Klein, Adler and Jung. Social work practice has been most heavily influenced by this approach, and it is not hard to see why. The emphasis is upon the relationship between feelings, emotions and behaviour and their roots in the unconscious life of individuals.

Freud and Erikson concentrated on questions about adult personality and developmental problems and crises, providing important knowledge for social workers. Melanie Klein's theories of infantile needs and experiences have been particularly popular in casework agencies such as the Family Welfare Association.

Here we will summarise Freud's theory of psychosexual development which preceeded other psychoanalytic work. He argued that all behaviour is characterised by instinctual drives or motivating forces. These can be divided into the libido, which is the sexual drive, the life preserving drives, and the aggressive drives. In Freud's view the sexual drives were the most important. Within each of us, he believed, is the need to seek gratification, and this process occurs throughout life.

Freud considered that there are three basic structures of personality that aid in gratifying the instincts. These are the id, ego and superego. The id is the original source of personality and contains everything that an individual inherits, the instinctual drives and the pleasure-seeking impulses. Like a young child, the id can be seen to operate according to the pleasure principle, avoiding pain and obtaining pleasure, regardless of external considerations. This basic push for gratification remains part of the personality, but with the experience that gratification can often be better achieved by a more considered approach to the external world, by planning and negotiating, the child gradually transfers energy from the id to the ego. This is the second structure to develop. The ego mediates between the demands of the id and the realities of life. The ego also mediates between the id and the superego, known collo-quially as the conscience. The superego, which enables individuals to decide between right and wrong, is the third structure to develop.

The ego is the mainly *conscious* part of the mind, and the id and superego are *unconscious*. these parts of the personality are seen as being in conflict, and the result of this conflict is anxiety. Most people experience anxiety which can often be directly handled by the ego. An example of this is the anxiety which surrounds the experience of being called out on a night duty visit to an unknown family, with the likelihood that a Place of Safety Order will be taken. This is a situation which calls for judgement – about the proba-bility that the family will be hostile to the social workers, the problems of liaising with the emergency children's reception centre and so on. The ego can handle this by looking objectively at the situation, realising its difficulties, recognising other people's likely anxieties, and mustering all one's professional skills in order to do the work as well as possible, bearing the child's needs in mind, rather than being swamped by anxiety.

However, sometimes there is too much anxiety to be handled by the ego, and individuals resort to 'defence mechanisms', Freud's term for unconscious strategies for reducing anxiety. Because these mechanisms are unconscious they involve self-deception, but they are quite normal, and part of everyone's experience. The defences can take the form of repression, rationalisation, projection, displacement, etc. So someone might repress the feelings surrounding a break-up in their marriage by insisting to themselves that nothing has gone wrong. Alternatively, she/he may rationalise that they never loved their partner anyway, and divorce would be the most sensible solution. Projecting anxiety would mean thinking of the partner as uncaring and unworthy of love, when in fact they fear those particular qualities in themselves. Finally, anxiety about the break-up of their marriage could be displaced by having arguments at work or being irritable with the children, and thus focusing attention on these 'problems', and away from the one which provokes too much anxiety.

In the course of development a child goes through a series of what Freud called psychosexual stages. The ego and superego develop during the course of these stages. Also the goals of gratification change according to the focus of the libido, which centres upon a particular part of the body, which he calls the erogenous zone, at each stage. These are the mouth, the anus and the genitals.

Freud proposed five stages. Between the age of 0–1 years of age, the infant goes through the oral stage, when the libidinal focus is on the mouth, tongue and lips. The major source of pleasure surrounds this area, and attachment to the mother is related to her being a source of oral pleasure. The anal stage occurs between the ages of 1–3 years. During this stage the baby is sensitive to the anal region of its body, which corresponds to the parents' efforts in toilet training. If toilet training becomes fraught, which it often does, Freud considered that a child might suffer to some extent for the rest of its life. The phallic stage takes place between the ages of 3 and 5. It is characterised by a shift away from the anal region towards the genital erogenous zone. At this stage both boys and girls may begin quite naturally to masturbate.

Freud said that an important event occurs during the phallic stage which he calls the oedipal conflict. Freud himself put more emphasis on the events related to boys' development, but parallel occurrences, he believed, take place for girls. He suggested that the boy becomes intuitively aware of his mother's sexuality, and at about the age of 4 begins to have a sort of sexual attraction to his mother and to regard his father as a sexual rival. He sees his father as having the ultimate power to castrate him, and thus the boy is caught between desire for his mother and fear of his father's power. The result of this conflict is anxiety, which he responds to with a process Freud calls identification. This means that he tries to make himself as much like his father as possible, and thus that he is taking on some of his father's powers too.

The related process which according to psychoanalytic theory occurs for girls is not described very well by Freud, who asserts that the girl sees her mother as a rival for her father's sexual attentions (although clearly she will not fear her mother's power so much as the boy fears his father's – perhaps bcause she assumes she has already been castrated) and because her anxiety is consequently weaker so is her identification.

The whole question of sex-typed behaviour, and parent-child relationships will be considered in Chapter 6. It is obviously an area of concern for all residential and field workers having to make relationships with children, and to make assessments of the families in which they are being brought up.

Freud considered that successful resolution of the oedipal crisis, by identification with the appropriate parent, is critical for healthy development, and any pattern of relationships and modes of behaviour in a family which would disrupt the identification process is severely problematic. An example might be a family in which the mother is more powerful than the father, creating severe problems for boys in the family. However, in the experience of many clients, the 'model' family as described by Freud must surely be rare. Keniston (1977) said that in the USA during the 1970s at least part of the childhood of four out of ten children would be spent with one parent only. The Finer Committee's 'Report on One Parent Families' (1974) showed a similarly high proportion in Britain. Thus it is important that social workers are able to accept and understand the relevant aspects of a theory, but also that they are able to modify and reject theories or parts of theories which are not useful. In Chapter 2, some attention will be paid to the previously dominant role psychoanalytic theory has played in social work practice. In subsequent Chapters, particularly 5, 6 and 7, complementary and alternative ways of looking at human relationships will be suggested.

Between the ages of 5 and 12, Freud says that children go through a period of latency without any major developmental changes. During these years the child's friends are almost exclusively of the same sex. In this period there is further development of the defence mechanisms, particularly those of denial (for instance, the child says that she/he is not tired when clearly unable to keep awake!), and repression, in which unacceptable thoughts and feelings are forced out of consciousness.

Between the ages of 12 and 18, and beyond, the adolescent's psychosexual stage corresponds with hormonal and biological changes, with the focus of interest on the genitals. The child is now interested in people of the opposite sex, with mature heterosexual love being the maturational goal. Clearly this is an assumption based upon an ideological view of mature sexuality; it demonstrates the way Freud himself perceived the world. Other psychoanalytic psychologists (e.g. Dinnerstein, 1976) have criticised this particular aspect of Freud's developmental theory and shown how homosexual love may also be considered a feature of normal development.

Social workers have understandably been interested in Freud's work because it is a major attempt to explain human development and human relationships which are of primary importance to the profession, but it is very difficult to *prove* many of Freud's assertions. Moreover they are value laden, with a particular view of sex-typed development and behaviour and of particular family patterns presented as the norm.

Behavioural psychology

Many social workers are now familiar with behaviour

modification, a therapeutic technique based upon knowledge derived from the behavioural school within psychology. This is one of the earliest approaches to understanding human behaviour, and was developed initially by Thorndike, Watson and Pavlov in the nineteenth century. Behaviourists are interested in questions relating to the conditions and events surrounding behaviour. For example, they are concerned with what actually happened *before* a person broke into tears, and what events took place in response to this. They feel that psychologists should limit themselves to *observable* events, and the ways in which behaviour is influenced by the environment. This is directly opposed to the psychoanalytic approach which concentrates on the inner and unconscious life of individuals, and stresses the significance of biology in determining development. Behaviourism is essentially an approach concerned with how individuals *learn* about the way in which they can best exist within their environment. Within the scope of this learning is included emotional development, perceptions of the external world, social behaviour and personality. Individuals learn by making connections between events in the environment, and two major theories have been developed concerning learning behaviour. These are classical conditioning and operant conditioning.

Studies of classical conditioning originated from the now famous work by Pavlov. He noticed that dogs salivated when they saw and smelled the food being brought to them. A bell was sounded just before the time that the food arrived, and Pavlov noticed that the dogs would eventually salivate on hearing the bell, even when there was no food to be seen or smelled. People also learn to anticipate relationships among stimuli, in order to make sense of the world. A child might learn that when her father has had too much to drink he hits her, and the pain makes her cry. Thus, when she hears her father returning from the pub she responds by bursting into tears. She has learnt that the combination of her father returning home and the place that he has been to indicate punishment for her. This is classical conditioning.

Operant conditioning occurs when an individual learns that some behaviour of his/her own leads to a particular *consequence.* A boy may take part in a range of activities at home, but when he plays with guns, and behaves in a typically 'masculine' way, his mother smiles at him. He therefore learns to behave in this way more frequently, as it gains his mother's approval. This process has been studied by Skinner, who demonstrated that behaviour in rats and pigeons can be 'conditioned' if responses are followed by 'reinforcement'. Reinforcements are the rewards or punishments which follow particular manifestations of behaviour. The mother smiling at the little boy's games is the reinforcement in the example. Conversely, a little girl playing with guns may have them taken from her, or be told with a frown that her behaviour is 'unladylike'. This acts as a punishment, and the child learns not to behave in that particular way.

Behaviour modification, mentioned earlier, is a method of helping a client change some form of undesirable and antisocial behaviour by offering rewards or punishments. For instance, mentally handicapped children often respond favourably to being cuddled or given sweets, and if they wash themselves or go to the toilet at the right time, they can be rewarded in that way. They learn to modify and adapt their behaviour as a means of obtaining the reward.

Social learning theory

During the 1960s Bandura developed social learning theory, which combines behavioural psychology and a cognitive approach taking more note of people's thoughts and perceptions (see next section). Social learning theory is particularly useful for looking at the way people learn their social behaviour.

Social learning is accomplished by using models (usually adults) whose behaviour is imitated by the children for whom that particular adult is important. It has been suggested that children model the behaviour of people who are warm and caring, which would include their parents, perhaps their favourite nursery teacher, or relatives. However psychologists have shown that this is not always the case, and that perhaps it is the *qualities* possessed by models rather than their place in the child's early life that makes them effective. Another important aspect of social learning theory and one which conflicts with psychoanalytic theory is that it is *observing* the model that is crucial, not necessarily interaction between the child and model.

The cognitive-developmental approach

This is a particularly relevant approach when considering aspects of socialisation (the way culture is transmitted from one generation to the next) as well as psychological development. (See Chapter 6 for a discussion of socialisation.) Cognitive-developmental psychology is concerned with the way people process information derived from both their internal world and the external world, and the way in which changes in the processing mechanisms occur.

The most influential psychologist in the area of cognitive development was Jean Piaget (1952). He suggested that it was not enough just to consider the child's behaviour, one had to look at the *quality of the thought processes* behind that behaviour. Also he found that children of different ages had different ways of thinking and solving problems. This perspective was at odds with the then current thinking, geared to intelligence-testing, which was concerned with the quantity of changes and development.

The central idea of Piaget's work, and that of other cognitive-developmental psychologists, is that every child is born with certain strategies for interacting with the environment. These strategies, which enable babies to make sense of their world in a particular way, are the starting points for the development of thinking. As children develop, so do their strategies – partly as a result of maturation, and partly as a result of the child's encounters with the external world. The discoveries the child makes about the world come about during the processes of development and exploration and occur in particular sequences. Thus there are certain things children are unable to do until they have grasped concepts which precede them (e.g. a child cannot grasp the idea of adding and subtracting until she has realised that objects are constant).

Piaget considered that the environment in which the child lives may affect the rate at which she goes through this development sequence, because the quality of experience is an important source of stimulation and mental exercise. However, as far as he was able to demonstrate, the environment does not enable children to miss out or skip stages in cognitive development.

An understanding of the concept of children's cognitive structure is especially important for residential workers faced with the task of ensuring that the children in their care make sesnse of their worlds, and the reasons why they are in care. It also provides a means of assessing children's responses to particular situations, as in the case of 'good' and 'bad' behaviour and moral reasoning (see Chapter 6).

Social psychology

Social psychology is different from the approaches described so far, partly because it incorporates a variety of psychological theories, but especially because it focuses upon the study of more than one person, and of individuals within the context of wider social groupings.

Social psychology is important for social workers most obviously because of mutual concern for social networks. In Chapter 4, aspects of group behaviour relevant to understanding family patterns and institutional life are examined, while in Chapter 7 there is a discussion of the social psychology of social work organisations.

Social psychology is both responsive to, and initiates change in conceptual and methodological issues.

In the 1970s there was a direct challenge to the positivist model of research (Harre and Secord, 1972) arguing that an understanding of the deeper levels of human encounter could only be assessed through analysis of subjective accounts of actions rather than objective measurement of interpersonal behaviour.

This line of attack upon mainstream psychology has been maintained and indeed strengthened through the work of *social constructionists* who argue for the understanding of human behaviour through the way individuals position themselves within existing discourses. This approach attempts to explain human experience (subjectivity) as an ideological venture rather than an essentially biological one, and so human social and individual actions might be understood as deriving from dominant social values rather than individual desires (see Kitzinger, 1987). This perspective is particularly important for social work practitioners grappling with the reasons why particular people appear to persist in what appear to be inappropriate behaviours.

The phenomenological or humanistic approach

This was developed largely by Kelly, Rogers and Maslow, who make the assumption that individuals have the motivation and ability to change, and are the best experts on themselves.

Humanistic psychology stresses the importance of freeing individuals from any barriers within themselves and between the self and the external reality. It also differs from other approaches in psychology, because of the value it attaches to subjective experience – that the individual's own view of the world *is* reality. The main concern therefore is how people perceive themselves and their surroundings, rather than with behaviour.

The central component of Rogers' theory is the self-concept. Someone with a positive self-concept views the world quite differently from someone whose self-concept is weak. The self-concept does not necessarily reflect reality – someone may be successful in the eyes of others, but see themselves as a failure. Rogers suggests that individuals have an 'ideal self', the person they would like to be, and that self-concepts of 'fully functioning' people are consistent or congruent with their thoughts, experience and behaviour (1978).

Feminism and psychology

Social and humanistic psychology have played some part

in encouraging the belated development of a feminist psychology. The scientific 'rigour' to which psychologists adhere is supposed to be 'value free' and thus any attempt to accuse it of a 'sexist bias', or to redress the balance by emphasising a *female* perspective in psychology has always been met with hostility from the (male) academic community. This is true both in the USA and UK, although North American psychologists have had a special division (Division 35) of the American Psychological Association, and an equivalent in Canada to study the psychology of women since the mid 1970s. In Britain it was not until 1987 that the British Psychological Society (BPS), after much debate, permitted the Psychology of Women Section to be formed (see Burman, 1989).

A feminist psychology of women is crucial for social work practitioners. It examines the way that 'psychology' has been (and still is for the most part) the 'psychology of men', so that developmental and behavioural issues specifically related to female psychology have been ignored and devalued. As social workers' clients are still more likely to be women (or under the care of women) and social workers themselves are also likely to be women, it seems appropriate that an accurate and sympathetic understanding of female psychology is essential, although not at the expense of the psychology of men.

Conclusions

Proposed changes and developments in social work qualifying courses, emphasising the practical experience component of training, have implications for the role of psychology. In many way the increased period of placement work demands that psychologists make their discipline more accessible to social work practitioners. It also means that social workers need to engage effectively with the psychological theories they are taught in the college environment. The burden of this must fall on the social work tutors who need to keep up to date with developments in psychology and employ psychological methods in their evaluation of social work practice and student performance. Further, there needs to be continued co-operation and interchange between applied psychologists working in the community and social work teachers and practitioners.

2

Psychology and Social Work

In the first edition of this book the history of psychology teaching on social work courses was discussed at some length, as it was through this that the estrangement between academic psychology and the psychodynamic interests of social work tutors was reflected.

Since the early 1980s many tutors trained in the psychodynamic tradition have retired or modified their approach in response to the demands of professional agencies who are now likely to be unable and unwilling to offer a casework service as in the 1960s model. The pressure is towards a more practical form of help in local authority departments dealing with community care initiatives, and more specialisation of approach in voluntary agencies.

In the meantime, academic psychology has begun to take psychodynamic psychology seriously (see for instance the BPS report on the Future of the Psychological Sciences, 1988) and the work of Freud and other psychoanalytic psychologists taught on undergraduate degrees.

What do social workers (and social work students) need to know from psychology?

(1) They need to know how to develop the social and psychological skills most useful in interviewing, and in assessing clients' needs.
(2) They need information about applied scientific research on relevant topics, as well as to have an ability to select what is relevant and apply it to the needs of the clients and organisations in which they work.

17

(3) Similarly they need to be able to make sense of these organisations in order to cope with their own career or professional development and training requirements.

(4) They need a thorough knowledge of human development in order to make such judgements and understand their colleagues and themselves. This is increasingly important as the stresses and strains and low morale precipitated by economic and political changes in the 1980s impinge upon social work practice and social workers' consciousness.

(5) They need to have enough knowledge of professional psychology to provide an effective and complementary service alongside clinical, educational and counselling psychologists.

In this book we have attempted to review the psychological knowledge that will inform social workers in these ways.

There are three levels of psychological knowledge which we employ in this and subsequent chapters: skills, theories and research evidence.

In discussing *skills*, we have concentrated on two main areas – interviewing and group work. Interviewing in this context is a social interaction between the professional worker and client, in which the interviewer obtains information and helps someone to come to a decision about their own problem. It also allows for information giving and advice. The interview is crucial because it is during this interaction that social work may be either effective or a waste of time.

Psychologists have studied counselling and assessment interviews, and used the data from these to develop models of good interviewing practice which have been developed and improved through trials with several professional groups (see Chapter 3).

There is an important difference between *skills* and psychological *knowledge* of human development, both of which are vital ingredients in successful social work interviews. In the case of reported child abuse, for instance, one aim of the interview would be to gain information. The social worker must establish the *facts* about the various incidents and emotional reactions in order to make judgements. He or she then has to make an assessment of the most suitable intervention for his or her agency. The perception of the events and future planning will depend upon the understanding of the family dynamics and its particular problems (through using knowledge of family interactions and human development). For the assessment to take place at all however, the social worker has to create the right conditions through conducting a good interview (or series of interviews). This is through communicating to the client that he or she is really listening and understanding; without which the client is unlikely to be able to express their true feelings and relevant details.

Similarly, when working with groups the social worker needs the skills to manage the group, which includes listening carefully and creating an environment conducive to group development. It also requires an understanding of the way groups develop and work on a conscious and unconscious level (see Chapter 4).

We employ psychological *theories* in order to understand wider aspects of a situation. Organisational processes, or psychological development for instance. In Chapter 7, theories or organisational psychology are applied to understanding work in teams and to residential care settings, and in Chapter 6, psychological theories applied to human development through the life cycle are employed so that any connections between age, stage and behaviour might be explained from within a theoretical framework rather than in an anecdotal or intuitive way.

There is also the psychological knowledge derived from scientific *research evidence* which often precedes the construction of a full theoretical explanation.

Recent work on children's memories and eyewitness testimony (e.g. Davies, 1988) has had an important practical effect within the legal system in cases of child abuse, and these changes are of immediate importance to both psychologists and social workers.

The emphasis in this book is on *applied* psychology for social workers, but we do want to stress that this means far more than skills. Research evidence and theory can and should be *applied* and social workers need to have an in-depth understanding of these.

To summarise, psychology may be applied to social work on three levels.

(1) At the level of immediate face-to-face encounter where *skills* in listening, demonstrating, understanding, presenting information clearly and concisely and so on, are of fundamental importance.

(2) At the level which requires *reflection* before, during and after action, where *understanding* based on psychological theory is applied. To understand why a member of a family is 'chosen' as scapegoat, or why certain individuals cannot seem to be able to work together, or why a residential home might be more suitable for one child than fostering, requires sympathy and human understanding but also the application of knowledge of human behaviour that has been gained in a systematic way.

(3) At the level of knowledge application. Here the social worker has to assess the facts of a problem and recall the facts of *reseach evidence* to make a judgement on how likely an individual might be to run away from home again, or whether family/couple work is more useful for a particular client than practical or financial help. This would be based on data referring to, for instance, personality or situational related behaviour, or the effects of stress.

Social work practice and applied psychology

To state that 'social work is a branch of applied psychology' (see Nicolson and Bayne, 1984) inflames the passions of representatives from both disciplines. There are a number of arguments which might lead an impartial observer to support this view, but for those involved a great deal of heart searching and qualification is required before the decision is reached that it is not!

Here, we want to examine the relationships between the two disciplines – the psychological knowledge base underpinning social work practice, and the relationship between professional psychologists and their social work counterparts.

Psychological knowledge and social work theory

Howe's (1987) overview of social work theory represents a departure from the previous psychodynamic or social policy/sociological emphases. He draws together, from a number of sources, theoretical knowledge that through innovation or adoption over time has become social work theory.

Relevant here is his reference to 'behavioural social work' and 'client centred approaches' without explicit acknowledgement of psychology. Does this mean that the boundaries between social work theory and psychological knowledge have become inescapably blurred?

While Hudson and MacDonald (1986) see behavioural social work as applying the principles of behaviourism and social learning theory to practice, Howe (1987) discusses behavioural social work as based on an understanding of concepts such as stimulus generalisation, operant conditioning, social learning, and modelling – but he does not mention the word 'psychology'. The *content* of his chapter on behavioural social work outlines what psychologists would identify as the source of modern scientific psychology, but Howe offers it as the source of behavioural social work.

Whether Pavlov, Watson or Skinner would bat an eyelid at this is of no consequence. What is interesting and important is whether or not the relationship between psychology and social work can and should be merged in this way.

Reading on we discover the 'client-centred' approach. Here Howe takes pains to introduce 'the natural psychologist', delivering a claim, for which he cites other writers also, that

> all human beings have an in-built aptitude for doing psychology. It is not just a clever thing to be able to do. It is a basic and necessary social skill given the sort of creatures that we are. (p. 107)

But what is 'doing psychology'? While it is important to argue, as we do throughout this book, that social workers and psychologists need to take subjective accounts of experience very seriously: being able to cope and communicate as a human being is *not doing psychology*. Psychology is a discipline with particular rules and methods which, although not without their critics, are tried and tested. More important, they are openly available to be further tried and tested in the tradition of scientific endeavour.

That psychology's 'absorption' is a justification of the importance of psychology to social work practice is not to advantage either discipline. A slight scratch on the surface of Howe's version of 'social work theory', as we have shown, reveals 'psychology'. To neglect to acknowledge the contribution of psychology to social work practice in this context prevents social work practitioners from making full use of wider principles and methods in psychology. The long tradition of psychology provides the basis of social work knowledge, and as such can operationalise concepts which are not obviously of concern in social work theory but, nevertheless, if applied correctly can inform social work. The following are illustrative of this.

Children's evidence

There is a tradition in experimental psychology of studying human memory and, more recently, its application in the case of eyewitness testimony. Concern with prosecution in child abuse and child sexual abuse cases has led to a positive relationship between experimental cognitive psychology and the practical and emotional problems and benefits for children giving evidence against their abusers.

The data derived from psychological research has led to the Home Office's commitment to the closed circuit TV link to the courtroom, so that a child may testify while physically outside. Without the child's testimony there are problems in securing convictions against abusers and, more important, it becomes more difficult to make plans for the future of the child.

Research has demonstrated that the trauma of a court-room appearance is potentially damaging as the original experience of abuse is re-created and the ensuing stress is likely to hinder memory as well as precipitate emotional disturbance (Davies, 1988).

Thus giving evidence outside the court is not just something that is 'more pleasant' for children. It is demonstrably more effective in obtaining truth and accuracy of recall.

Additional recommendations based on psychological research indicate the importance of a 'trusted intermediary' (probably a social worker known to the child) to be employed to assist in the questioning procedure rather than an unknown court official (Davies, 1988).

The psychology of disasters

Another source of stress which concerns both psychologists and social workers is in the area of 'disasters'.

Clegg (1988) points out that 1987 was designated (retrospectively) the 'Year of Disaster', based on the capsize of the Herald of Free Enterprise, motorway accidents, the worst storm of the century and bombings in Ulster. Since then there have been even more, with several football stadium disasters and the community of Lockerbie devastated by a plane crash.

Social workers are faced with the immediate emergencies, but also with the task of picking up the pieces long after the media have retreated. Psychological research has provided a 'profile' of the disaster victim's experience indicating a 'post traumatic stress disorder' (PTSD) which may prevent someone from being able to lead a normal life for a period of years. This disorder presents further problems for family members – both financial and emotional – including management of the grief process, which is complicated by the victim's survival.

This research is new, but based on psychological theory and psychological methods of investigation. It also begs for the co-operation of social work practitioners in a joint effort to explore the parameters and consequences of disasters on individuals, families and communities.

Feminism and psychology

Feminist studies of the psychology of women (see Wilkinson, 1986; Ussher, 1989) have enabled a totally new set of perspectives upon human development and behaviour to become available to social work practitioners and although social workers might claim a prior feminist consciousness, the systematic collection and application of knowledge of female psychology have had direct consequences for social work practitioners which stimulate and inform feminist practice.

Ussher enables practitioners to reconceptualise women's relationship with the 'raging hormones' and to consider whether medical responses to post-natal depression or the menopause are the most appropriate.

Wilkinson draws together differences in morality, attitudes to the life cycle, the experience of being a lesbian, childbirth, growing older and so on – none of which are readily available in traditional 'scientific' psychology.

Finally, research and co-operation between social workers and psychologists is well reported in cases of domestic violence, and child sexual abuse, and provides examples of why this joint research and practice should continue (e.g. Glaser and Frosh, 1988).

The relationship between applied psychologists and social workers

Occupational, clinical and educational psychologists have long established career structures in Britain and the USA. More recently, counselling psychology has become a recognised area of applied expertise and some traditionally trained psychologists have also had further training in psychoanalysis, family therapy and of course social work, which is a popular choice among psychology graduates wanting a more 'human' application of their discipline than that offered by experimentation and measurement. This has led to the formation of a working party among professional psychologists (answering to the BPS Professional Affairs Board) to examine the future of the various branches of professional psychology and its relationship with its professional allies.

Social work practice and psychological theory

Much of what social workers actually do works despite the well publicised problems where social workers have been presented by the media as incompetent.

Many argue that social work is intuitive – a craft (Maas, 1980, cited by Herbert, 1981) and as such relies on suitable individuals who are 'high in sensitivity and concern for others but low in logical thinking and intellectual discrimination' to carry out its tasks.

There is no evidence that this is the case. Social workers do indeed need to have concern for the welfare of others as part of their work; but it is impossible to achieve welfare in a universal sense – so there is rarely a situation in which every participant benefits. Social workers (whatever their employing agency) have well defined duties and powers, and within these there are tightly defined boundaries.

Intuition is based on prejudice (see Chapter 5) and is not the most effective, nor the most empathic way of changing people's lives. It is just such human difficulties that have inspired and justified psychological research, most recently into the areas of violence and sexual abuse and the related areas of child witnesses.

It is because social work practitioners acknowledge the need to have access to scientific information about human performance, human development, pathology and so on, that psychologists have been asked to conduct research into these areas. It is because social workers are being asked to place mentally handicapped and long-term ex-psychiatric patients in the community that research into normalisation and stress in the family is being funded. It is because social

workers are having to account for themselves and re-
evaluate how they spend their time, that psychologists are
being commissioned to evaluate a number of programmes
run by local authorities and other social work agencies.

The relationship between psychology and social work
then is highly productive but demands mutual respect and
awareness. For social workers to ignore psychology or to
take it for granted will lead to inadequate knowledge and
practice. Similarly psychologists involved in teaching social
workers or doing research into areas of social work should
have a detailed and sympathetic knowledge of the social
work role.

3

Interviewing and Counselling

Introduction

Much of a social worker's time is spent talking and listening to clients and colleagues. While some of these conversations, meetings and interviews go well, most people can think of times when the outcome could have been better in some way, when they perhaps felt baffled or frustrated by the lack of communication. This chapter discusses some of the skills and qualities involved in communicating effectively, particularly when interviewing and counselling, but also in other kinds of conversation. It is intended to help you work on your skills and on yourself.

To try to make clear distinctions between interviewing and counselling is to enter a quagmire. However, Ivey *et al.* (1987) suggest the following, which will be used to structure the sections on interviewing and counselling. With many qualifications, they define interviewing as 'a method of information gathering' and counselling as 'a more intensive process concerned with assisting normal people to achieve their goals or function more effectively' (p. 18). They note that the two terms and a third term, psychotherapy, are often used interchangeably, and that the overlap between all three is considerable, e.g. 'Counselors may conduct therapy, they often interview as well. While concerned with normality, they often work with clinical issues' (p. 19).

The chapter is in five sections. The first section focuses on interviewer and counsellor training, with a brief discussion of research on the effectiveness of counselling, and suggestions on how to use the rest of the chapter. The remaining four sections discuss and outline in a practical way four sets of skills:

(1) Interviewing, in the sense of information-gathering;
(2) counselling, placing the interviewing skills in a model of counselling based on Egan (1986);
(3) assertiveness, and
(4) psychological self-care.

There are also two appendices, the first some suggestions for coping with difficult aspects of interviewing and counselling, and the second a checklist for analysing interviews and counselling sessions.

Interviewer and counsellor training

One answer to the question 'why bother with training?' is that it is usually in interviews, or as a result of interviews, that specialist knowledge is used. Good interviewing skills and qualities make it more likely to be used well. There are also other benefits: for example, clients are more likely to feel listened to (and for good reason); interpersonal skills are associated with better physical and mental health (e.g. Duck, 1983; 1986); being interviewed for a job or 'appraisal' should be more fruitful. They are not, however, a cure for everything!

A second reason is that considerable improvements in skill can be achieved relatively easily. Maguire and Rutter (e.g. Maguire, 1981) provide particularly strong evidence. They were concerned with improving communications between doctors and patients, and in particular with the initial history, i.e. doctors gathering accurate and relevant information from a patient new to them. They began by studying videotapes of such interviews between senior medical students and patients and found numerous deficiencies – including failure to pick up cues, repetition (which at best is a waste of time), asking leading questions and, perhaps ironically, acceptance of jargon, e.g. taking at face value a statement like 'I feel depressed'. The results were very clear, e.g. 74 per cent of the students were rated as poor or very poor at picking up verbal leads, while 24 per cent failed to discover the patient's main problems – and this with patients who were chosen as co-operative and articulate.

Maguire and Rutter's next step was to devise a training programme, a 45- to 60-minute individual tutorial for each student in which one of her or his interviews was replayed and discussed, and compared with the information which should have been obtained. A handout on interview structure and technique was also discussed with reference to the replayed interview. Maguire and Rutter's evaluation of the training compared the amount of relevant and accurate information obtained by trained and untrained students respectively. Again the results were very clear: the trained students obtained nearly three times as many relevant items of information. On this evidence, interviewer training is necessary, desirable and highly cost-effective.

Matarazzo and Patterson (1986) similarly conclude that counselling skills training, using a variety of methods, appears to be effective. A related, but far more complex question, is 'Does counselling work?' It is very important, ethically and financially, to know. Do some approaches or methods actually do harm? Do some of the cheaper or quicker approaches work just as well as others? The answer to both these questions appears to be yes, as indeed it is to the general question (Stiles *et al.*, 1986). Counselling does work. However, not much is known yet about *why* it works, or which elements and approaches are the most effective in which situations.

One of the problems with research on counselling effectiveness is that there are about 200 approaches to counselling (Ivey *et al.*, 1987). Only a few of the approaches have been studied in any detail and few people know, or have even heard of, all of them. However, there have been thousands of studies of counselling, and several major reviews of the studies to try and make sense of the variety of counsellor, client, problem, method etc. involved, and there is fairly general agreement that the main approaches work about equally well for most purposes. This is an extraordinary position. One reaction to it is that it is untrue, that some approaches have yet to be fairly tested or cannot be tested.

A second reaction is to look for 'common ingredients'. Two of the many possibilities are particularly relevant to the approach discussed in this chapter: the so-called 'core qualities' and a judicious mixture of support (or 'warm involvement') and challenge (or 'communicating a new perspective on client or situation').

The 'core' qualities (empathy, respect and genuineness) have also been studied extensively. Patterson (1984) reviewed the reviews of research on them and showed – not surprisingly – that the reviewers were biased in the studies they chose to include and their treatment of those studies, applying higher standards of criticism to those whose conclusions they disagreed with, overlooking flaws in those they agreed with.

For example, in one study 75 'person-centred' counsellors were investigated – a huge number. But the 75 were only 5 per cent of those invited, and thus a very biased sample. Moreover, almost all were rated as *low* on the three qualities. The study found few positive relationships between the qualities and effectiveness and – despite the flaws – has been cited as evidence against their potency. According to Patterson the more than 500 studies are generally flawed, but he argues that the flaws to some extent cancel each other out. In his view the qualities emerge with strong support: they are *necessary* conditions for effective counselling, and sometimes *sufficient*. This view is consistent with the model of counselling discussed later in this chapter.

In broad terms, I suggest the following implications of research on the outcome of counselling for practitioners:

(1) Try out a range of approaches;
(2) choose to specialise in those which seem to 'fit' you best;
(3) examine both your 'successes' and your 'failures' with clients critically and constructively, and some of the time with others (supervision, case discussion);

(4) look out for research findings. For example, Greenberg and Dompierre (1981) show that two chair technique (from Gestalt counselling) is generally more effective than active listening on its own for helping someone make a difficult decision. Consider incorporating such findings into your own approach, and

(5) respond with care to claims of effectiveness, especially of therapeutic wizardry, as well as to dismissals such as 'It's just talking'.

The 'core' qualities and a skills approach

The 'core' qualities or attitudes for effective counselling are discussed in detail by many writers (e.g. Rogers, 1961; 1978), Gilmore (1973), Egan (1986) and Mearns and Thorne (1988). *Empathy* can be defined as 'showing that you understand the client's feelings and see the client's point of view' – with the emphasis on 'showing', and in a specific way; *genuineness* as 'being yourself' – though 'appropriately' rather than bluntly or unflinchingly; and *respect* as 'warm acceptance of the other person' – though some clients respond best to a matter-of-fact kind of warmth. The comments after each brief definition hint at some of the complexities. Moreover, the core qualities are given a variety of names and definitions, and other qualities have been suggested, e.g. composure and a willingness to discuss everything (Brenner, 1982), tolerance – lack of a need for perfection – and discretion (Reddy, 1987).

In this chapter the core qualities are, in effect, defined as skills. There is a problem with this. Skills used in a genuine, personal way (i.e. by someone who has developed the core qualities) are more likely, by definition, to contribute to a more authentic relationship and therefore, in most theories of counselling, to change. Conversely, use of the skills without the qualities is mechanical and hollow. Some writers have no place for a skills approach. Thus Rogers (1987) commented on training people to 'reflect feelings': 'It does not describe what I am trying to do when I work with a client. My responses are attempts to check my understanding of the client's internal world. I wish to keep an accurate up-to-the minute sensitivity to his or her inner searchings, and the response is an endeavour to find out if I am on course with my client' (p. 39).

My view is that skills training is sometimes superficial and that interviewing and counselling are in some respects mysterious and not captured at the level of skills. A sense of timing for example is part of their artistic side, but the term 'timing' is more a question than an explanation. On the other hand, skills training and personal development can be seen as complementing each other, with the skills giving a more systematic framework for analysis: used well, the skills outlined here both communicate the qualities and also aid their development. Other approaches to developing self-awareness (the key quality) are discussed in the section on psychological self-care.

Using this chapter

This chapter is intended to help you analyse your own interviews and other conversations in a constructive way. It supplements training courses and supervision. In this section the approach to this self-training and the meaning of 'constructive' are elaborated with some general principles, and some suggestions about 'feedback'. The principles are:

(1) Good interviewing and counselling have a large element of individual style (as genuineness implies). The skills are not meant to be used mechanically. It follows that the skills sections contain suggestions to consider and try out rather than prescriptions.
(2) Everyday conversations give lots of opportunities for practising the skills, and some opportunities for observing them. They 'belong to life' as Egan put it and are not magical (though their effects can seem so). Moreover, you are probably good at some of the skills already. The assumption here though is that all interviewers and counsellors, whatever their training and experience, can usefully review their existing skills,

and try out new ones – and indeed need to do so in order to develop.

(3) Improvement may not happen all at once, or in a smooth progression. It may well involve feeling self-conscious and awkward for a while but, as with developing other skills, (e.g. driving, playing a sport or cooking), the skills feel 'right' and natural in time. For most skills, it takes a lot of time, practice and appropriate feedback to achieve virtuoso standard: Norman (1982) estimates 5000 hours (from talking to ice-dancers, snooker players, etc.). Fortunately there is improvement meanwhile, and it is not necessary to be a virtuoso to be effective.

Giving 'feedback' to yourself. To give 'feedback' is to comment to someone on how well you think they have done something. Here it refers more specifically to commenting on how well you think you have communicated the core qualities and used interviewing and counselling skills.

The following principles are general guidelines; as with counselling there are no absolute rules. Please note too that giving feedback is a *skill*, and therefore develops with appropriate practice.

● Comment on behaviour, and try to be fairly specific, e.g. 'I seemed very relaxed – I think it was the way I sat and my use of silence.' (The comment could be more specific still, but this is probably sufficient.)
● Include positive comments.
● Criticise behaviour that could be changed and try to say what you might do differently: one or two things at a time only.
● Be brief: three or four comments at the most.

The principles suggested then are to be specific, positive as well as critical, constructive and brief.

Information-gathering

Two sets of skills are distinguished. In practice they

overlap, but the division is useful. The first set of skills is primarily for building a relationship and for gathering information (the emphasis in interviewing) or helping someone explore (emphasis in counselling). They are often referred to as 'supporting skills'. Those considered here are: basic listening, negotiating a contract, asking questions, paraphrasing or basic empathy, concreteness, silence and summarising. The second set of skills is primarily for testing the accuracy of the information gathered, if that is necessary. They include advanced empathy and immediacy and are often referred to as 'challenging skills'. Two other skills are also considered: preparation for an interview, and keeping a record.

Preparation

Preparing for an interview can include thinking about the following factors: the time available, what you hope to achieve, whether your aims conflict with those of others e.g. organisations, a broad structure for the interview, and what information might be useful. A straightforward structure would be 'Introduce myself. Find out about X. Find out about Y. Agree on action.' A structure is a checklist of aims and topics, and perhaps an opening question for each topic. The possible aims include gathering information (for one or more specific purposes), giving information, helping someone to make a decision or to behave differently. There is also a 'public relations element' – the term is perhaps unfortunate, but how interviewers are seen by their clients matters – e.g. it affects whether clients see you in the first place and whether they continue to see you.

Clearing your mind of distractions is another aspect of preparation. Argyle (1978) describes the 'right frame of mind for an interview' (for all participants) as an 'undivided attention' which is conducive to an 'atmosphere of timeless calm'. Relaxation exercises are one possible way of approaching somewhat nearer to 'timeless calm' than normal, for instance this breathing exercise:

(1) First make yourself comfortable. Take two or three deep breaths through your nose. Then place one of your index fingers on the point between your eyebrows, with the thumb on one nostril, middle finger on the other.

(2) Closing your left nostril, breathe in slowly and deeply through the right.

(3) Closing your right nostril, breathe out slowly through the left.

(4) Keeping right nostril closed, breathe in through the left.

(5) Closing left nostril, breathe out through the right.

You can breathe in to (say) a count of three, hold for two, out to six – but ideally find your own rhythm. A further refinement of the instructions is that when you've breathed out, pause and wait until you want to breathe in – until it 'feels right'.

This simple device has not been tested experimentally yet. Benson (1977) describes a similar procedure which has been tested and which, like many exercises, works well for some people. He sees it as meditation without the unnecessary trappings, and calls it the 'relaxation response'. It is less useful than alternate nostril breathing in at least two respects: it takes longer and it appears to work less well after meals. The procedure is as follows:

(1) Sit quietly in a comfortable position and close your eyes.

(2) Deeply relax all your muscles, beginning at your feet and progressing up to your face, by tensing and relaxing each part of your body in turn or by 'playing dead'.

(3) Breathe through your nose. As you breathe in say the word 'one' to yourself. Continue for 10 minutes. When you finish, sit quietly.

(4) Do not worry about success in being relaxed: allow relaxation to occur at its own pace. Expect other thoughts. When they occur ignore them by thinking 'oh well' and continue repeating 'one'.

(5) Practise this procedure once or twice daily, but not until two hours after a meal.

Further aspects of preparation are (again, ideally) having a quiet room with no interruptions, and knowing that the client has waited, if at all, in pleasant surroundings. Such factors do not guarantee a good interview but they probably increase the chances of one. The interviewer might also consider what if anything she or he knows about the clients, and therefore what legislation, agencies and other resources are relevant.

Negotiating a 'contract'

In the interview itself, negotiating a contract is a useful first step. The contract is a concise statement about the purpose of the interview and a request for the other person's response or for what they see as the purpose. For example, 'I'd like to find out as much as possible about your experience with children. We have about 30 minutes. I'd like to take notes, which will, of course, be confidential. Is that OK?' The interviewer might also say to the client: 'Can you begin by saying why you've come to see me?', or 'What do you hope will happen as a result of this meeting?' There may be a significant gap between what the client expects and what the social worker can provide. Possible elements for the contract include: time available, place, number of meetings, resources, style/process, confidentiality, note-taking etc. It is vital to be clear about your own intentions, to listen very carefully to the client, and for there to be genuine agreement before proceeding. Some elements may not be negotiable, so the skill is also concerned with setting boundaries.

The advantages of negotiating a contract are numerous. The interviewer is likely to become less mysterious and threatening. The ground is cleared and a purposeful tone is set. If agreement is genuine, both people are more likely to take part wholeheartedly. If you do not reach agreement, at least some time is saved.

In outline the basic skill is straightforward:

(1) Say what you would like to do, etc. and/or ask the other person to say what they would like to do.

(2) Listen.
(3) Agree if possible. You or the client may modify your perceptions or intentions in the light of the other person's intentions. The skill can be used for re-negotiating or clarifying at any point in the interview.
(4) Check the contract from time to time and be ready to re-negotiate.

Basic listening

Basic listening (called 'attending' by Egan) is partly giving fairly straightforward non-verbal 'messages': looking at the client, but not staring; being fairly relaxed; nodding slowly; smiling (if appropriate); not fidgeting. And it is partly internal: avoiding distractions and concentrating (hence the relaxation exercise). One problem with attention can be also a strength. The average rate of speech is about 125 to 75 words a minute, but we can think much faster. The difference can be used to daydream, to worry, to think about anything at all, or it can be used to attend to such questions as 'What is the client not saying?', 'What about the client's non-verbal behaviour?', 'What about mine?', 'Where is the interview going at the moment?', 'What are the aims?', 'Time to summarise?'.

Asking questions

There are various categories of question but the most useful distinction is probably between open and closed questions. Open questions invite the client to talk at greater length if she/he wants to, e.g. 'Tell me about X', 'What's hap-pened?', 'Mmmm . . .', and perhaps less obviously: 'In what way?' and 'Can you say how?'. They encourage clients to give an overview, and thus the interviewer is likely to gather better information.

Closed questions on the other hand are easy to answer with one word. Moreover, a series of closed questions soon sounds like an interrogation, with the client more likely to leave information out because 'he was not asked'. More subtly, in using a series of closed questions the interviewer is saying in effect, 'I know what is important and relevant. I will ask the questions. I will come up with a solution', when (especially in counselling) both interviewer and client should be actively working on the problem.

Open questions give space and involvement while closed questions help place the client in a dependent relationship. They use the interviewer's framework more than the client's, thus hindering empathy. The most effective pattern, generally, is to ask one or more open questions on a particular topic, and then if necessary follow up with closed questions, e.g. to check a piece of information: 'Was that *two* or *three* months ago?'

Some examples of open questions are: What kinds of things have you tried? When do you feel best about yourself? What might happen if you did that? A variation is to take a word or phrase the client has said and reflect it back: 'Tired?' What might be called delayed reflections are a further variation. The interviewer remembers a phrase or word the person used earlier, and ties it in with something they have just said, but relatively gently and tentatively rather than as an interrogation. 'Why' questions are open but may lead to the client feeling attacked, or making up an answer to please you. (Like all 'rules' of interviewing this is only generally so.) Consider the difference between 'Why are you scared of going to the doctor?' and 'Can you say what scares you about . . .?'

Many other forms of question have been suggested, e.g. leading questions like 'I suppose you're sorry now?', which are both closed and suggest the 'right' answer. Dillon (e.g. in Hargie, 1986) reviews research on questions and their effects in all kinds of settings. Simple and apparently trivial differences in wording have dramatic effects. General principles for interviewers are to ask fewer questions, to prepare opening questions carefully, and to let what the client says influence strongly any follow-up questions.

Concreteness

Concreteness means 'asking for relevant detail' or asking

someone to be more specific, e.g. 'Can you give me an example?' or 'Depressed?'

Paraphrasing (basic empathy)

All the skills outlined so far can have strong effects, out of all proportion to the way they appear. This is particularly true of paraphrasing (called 'basic empathy' by Egan (1986) and sometimes called restating, rephrasing or active listening). It is the single most powerful communication skill in most professional circumstances, because it clears up more miscommunication than any other skill. It is described here in a number of sections. The idea is not to hold all of these in mind while interviewing someone but to practise on the lines of the first section below, preferably with feedback, e.g. from a tape-recorder or supervision group, and to *gradually* try out other aspects.

The basic skill

A paraphrase re-states what someone has said:
—Using fewer words;
—using (generally) your own words, thus avoiding sounding like a parrot or a computer;
—trying to give a sharper focus, to say it in a fresh way.

The most basic form of paraphrase is 'You feel . . . (feeling) because of . . .'. The tone is slightly questioning without being a question.

Paraphrase quite frequently, interrupting if necessary. Gendlin (1981) suggests – very roughly – every 5 sentences or so when listening to a difficult problem. In everyday conversations, an occasional paraphrase is more appropriate.

Paraphrases which include a feeling are rare in everyday conversations. Instead we comment, persuade, interpret, sympathise, reassure, question, paraphrase content except for feelings ('what you're saying is'), or change the subject.

Purposes of paraphrasing

● Helps you to listen more carefully.
● Shows both you and the other person – in a very direct way – how well you've listened. Builds trust. Shows you are not afraid of feelings.
● Enables the other person to correct any misunderstanding, to clarify and/or to explore further.

How do you know when you're paraphrasing well? (Adapted from Gendlin, 1981)

The other person is more likely to:

—say more, and in a more open way;
—say 'Yes', 'That's right', etc. (with some conviction);
—sit silently, satisfied that you've understood. 'I don't have to say *that* any more'. May take a deep breath and relax.

How do you know when you're paraphrasing badly?

The other person is more likely to:

—repeat what he/she has said already;
—look puzzled and perhaps try to understand *you*;
—change the subject, especially to something less personal;
—become annoyed. 'I've just said that.'
—Agree in a passive way.

Some guidelines

● 'Feeling paraphrases' label feelings which the other person has stated or clearly implied. If you guess a feeling (or anything else) that's not paraphrasing. Cf. p. 45.
● Use simple words.
● Focus on the other person's experience or reaction, not on the problem or on anyone else the person is talking about.

Some subtle aspects of paraphrasing

● If you're not aware of your own feelings and thoughts,

you are likely to confuse them with the other person's. Paraphrasing reveals this error.

Try pausing to consider, before paraphrasing – you may be briefer then too.

The way you speak and your expression etc., should 'go with' your words, e.g. 'You're furious with . . .' said a *bit* angrily rather than with a smile or in a mechanical or wooden way.

Examples of words which label feelings are 'angry', 'delighted' and 'like'. 'You feel you should do it' labels a thought not a feeling.

Pause after a feeling has been recognised, to allow the other person to feel it more.

Different kinds of feeling can be distinguished (Greenberg and Safran, 1989), some of which it may be more useful to focus on than others.

Generally, do not paraphrase when:

—you don't want the other person to say more or to 'feel' listened to;
—he or she genuinely wants information or ideas – though it still sometimes helps to check what about first;
—your values are challenged too strongly;
—you are tired or preoccupied.

Three risks of paraphrasing

By showing someone that you see their point of view you may change your own.

The other person may be too open too quickly, for them or for you, and regret it later.

You may use paraphrasing to avoid being aware of or expressing your own feelings and thoughts. (See sections on self-awareness, p. 53, and assertiveness, p. 51.)

An attractive aspect of paraphrasing is that it is difficult to fake. To paraphrase so that the client says 'Yes, that's exactly right, that is how I feel', the interviewer has to understand too. It is far more than the interviewer saying

'Yes, I see what you mean', or 'I understand how you feel' (which may mean 'I know how I feel in that situation').

Perhaps the most difficult aspect to learn is accurately paraphrasing depth of feeling. However, it may be that initial accuracy can be over-emphasised: Gendlin (1981) suggests successive approximations, gradually getting closer, as a more realistic aim, with the interviewer expecting to be *wrong* at first. 'Accuracy' is defined at this stage by the client: it is whether the paraphrase feels right to him or her that matters.

Another way of looking at paraphrasing and the other skills of active listening is to contrast them with other kinds of response. Suppose someone says 'I feel so hopeless. My children don't listen. I've no money. My wife is hardly here and when she is she just sits or we argue. We don't go anywhere. I used to like going out with her.' You may like to pause here and imagine your response. The first 8 responses listed below are *not* examples of active listening:

(1) To move quickly on to another subject.
(2) To say 'Nonsense', or 'You don't really mean that'.
(3) To offer advice: 'If I were you . . .'.
(4) To sympathise: 'I know just how you feel . . .', or 'I feel the same way sometimes . . .', or 'Lots of people feel like that . . .'.
(5) To offer practical help: 'Why don't you come out with me?'
(6) To blame society etc.
(7) To diagnose: 'When do you feel this way?' or 'How long have you been married?'
(8) To attack: 'People like you . . . You make me . . .?'
(9) To paraphrase, e.g.: 'You sound despairing and a bit sad'.
(10) To reflect: 'Hopeless?' (very gently).

Consider a similar range of responses to a parent saying 'The baby cried all night. I came close to hitting him. I want to have a life of my own. I'm so fed up', and to a client who says: 'You're a lot of pompous do-gooders. I despise you. You're no use to anyone except your own kind.

I don't know how you can live with yourselves, why don't you do a proper job?'

What responses 1 to 8 above have in common is that they do not encourage clients to explore their thoughts and feelings further, from *their* point of view. On some occasions they are helpful (Hopson, 1981a) but in a fundamentally different way from paraphrasing which says, in effect, 'I want to see your point of view, as a first step'. With enough practice, basic empathy will seem at least as natural as offering opinions and advice, or asking questions, or other responses. It *is* natural in the sense that some people do it without formal training.

Silence

Interviewers are sometimes afraid of silence and rush to fill the gap. Generally it is more skilful to wait, and try to assess why the client has stopped talking. Reasons include:

● because there is nothing more they wish to say about a particular topic;
● to organise thoughts/look for the right word;
● to remember something;
● feeling angry, defensive, confused, etc.

The kind of silence (productive, peaceful, rejecting and so on) suggests which skill to employ. Silence itself is usually appropriate for the second and third reasons listed above. Otherwise, paraphrase, ask an open question, summarise or use 'immediacy' (p. 46).

Summarising

Summaries serve the same purposes as paraphrases and also have a flavour of 'This is where we are so far. What's next?'

Gilmore (1973) suggests several other techniques for 'moving an interview forward'. Used when the relationship between you is a relatively trusting one, the techniques (a) communicate respect and empathy (Gilmore's terms are, respectively, acceptance and understanding), (b) help the client explore one thing at a time, and (c) increase the client's sense of control (or reduce a sense of being overwhelmed).

Three techniques are outlined below, using for illustration the position of John, a colleague who has asked you for advice. John is upset and doesn't know what to do. He is behind with a major report and wonders about changing jobs. One friend says there are other, better jobs. Another says he will be sorry if he leaves. His boss is very busy at the moment, but has said to 'get something on paper and then we can discuss it'.

Formulating a choice point. This is a summary by the interviewer plus an open question about which aspect to explore further. For example, speaking to John the interviewer might say: 'Of these problems – the pressure of getting your report done, feeling uncertain about staying in this job, your confusion about the differing views of your friends, resenting your boss – which would you like to look at first'. Other possible expressions include 'Which could we start working on now?' and 'Which do you think it would be helpful to talk about first?' Essentially, a choice point offers the client an open choice of which area to explore further. This may not be the area *you* think best (or most interesting!).

Gaining a figure ground perspective. Figure ground also includes a summary but then it is the counsellor who suggests which aspect to explore further. An example is the same summary as above plus '. . . Perhaps your main worry is the report . . .? Other possibilities include 'What seems to be most important to you is . . .' or 'Shall we talk first about . . .?' Criteria for choice of area include a problem that might be managed relatively easily (giving experience of success and sense of movement) or a problem that affects others.

Requesting a contrast. This is again a summary, this time with a hypothetical question. The aim is to clarify the client's *present* feeling, however, rather than to speculate, or to escape from the present. For example (to John): 'You feel miserable at work and everyone's advice is different. Let's imagine you'd finished your report and were pleased with it. How would that feel?' Alternative expressions include, 'How would that feel differently from now?' and 'Would any of your other difficulties look different?'

Challenging skills

Challenging skills deliberately introduce a new perspective on the client's problem. They come from *your* frame of reference or at least from a way of looking at something or feeling about it which is different from the client's. This is of course in marked contrast to supporting skills, which attempt to stay in the client's frame of reference. For example, 'advanced empathy' is sharing a hunch about how the client is feeling when they seem to you unaware of the feeling. This is risky. The risk is reduced by 'earning the right' to challenge, i.e. by empathising with the client first, by challenging tentatively, and by returning to supporting skills immediately after challenging (i.e. you introduce a new perspective and then listen hard and actively to the client's reaction).

The other challenging skills include *confronting* – suggesting themes or patterns, or someone else's point of view, or asking the client how someone else sees it, or pointing to an apparent discrepancy; *self-disclosure* – revealing something personal with the intention of helping the client or the relationship; using a *technique* from another approach to counselling, e.g. from gestalt or cognitive; and *giving information*. As an example of the effect of a piece of information, I remember reading that my badly sprained ankle was equivalent to a broken one and at once feeling much more patient with how long it was taking to heal. My feelings of impatience and frustration were transformed by this new way of looking at my injury.

For practical guidelines on 'informational care' – reducing the distress caused by poor or indeed no information –

see Nicholls (1984). Ley (1988) suggests ways of giving complicated information so that it is more likely to be remembered and acted on, though 'adherence' would be a less authoritarian term than 'compliance' (Harvey, 1988). The main guidelines, based on extensive research, are: use simple words and short sentences, categorise explicitly, be specific (concrete), avoid jargon, repeat and provide written back-up material.

Immediacy is probably the most difficult challenging skill. It overlaps with being assertive to a large extent. One form of immediacy is sharing your experience of what is happening at that very moment between you and the client, and encouraging the client to do the same. It is 'direct, mutual talk', and you are both involved; the focus is on you and the relationship rather than just on the client. Some examples: 'I feel stuck, as if we're going round in circles. What do you think?'; 'I'm feeling uncomfortable about the way we're talking. There's something not right. How do you see it?'; 'I see us as playing something of a game. I think that I've fallen into suggesting various solutions, with you seeing flaws in each one?'

Keeping a record

Writing a report – for yourself or others – helps clarify thinking. The stages of a counselling model (next section) provide an obvious structure.

Part of the value of a structure is that it suggests relevant aspects of people or problems which may have been missed or insufficiently emphasised in the interview. It also encourages questions about the process of interviewing, e.g. 'What stage is the relationship at?', 'Where is it going?' and 'What skills did I use?' This possibility is more systematically illustrated in the checklist (Appendix 1). Gilmore (1973, pp. 123–32) describes a framework for describing clients and their situations, Tallent (1983) discusses the skill of writing psychological 'case' reports, with attention to Barnum statements (discussed with other ideas about evidence for judgements of personality in

Chapter 5 here). Danbury (1986, Chapter 5) reviews purposes, methods and the special case of court reports in a clear and practical way. McMaster (in Hargie, 1986) also offers some valuable suggestions. General issues which need to be considered include 'Why are records kept?' and 'Who has access to them?'

Counselling: Egan's 1986 Model

Introduction

In this section, I discuss Egan's most recent (1986) model of counselling or 'problem management'. He used the latter term to emphasise the point that some problems cannot be solved in any complete sense, but that all problems can be managed. As with the skills, the idea is for you to try out those parts of the model which make sense to you, and 'fit' you, and to do this gradually and systematically, i.e. practice with analysis/feedback as described on p. 33. The model will either clarify part of what you do already, and perhaps crystallise it, or suggest new aspects of counselling to integrate into your own style.

This process of developing and refining your approach to counselling makes use of the best thinking of others. In counselling, it is a life-long process (BAC Code of Ethics, 1985; Ivey *et al.*, 1987). Two analogies may be helpful. One is *beachcombing* (Egan uses 'mining'; a perhaps less attractive term is scavenging) among books, tapes, conferences, journals, etc. for ideas and techniques. The second is *savaging* what you find: really working on it until either it contributes to your own approach or you discard it. The same savaging applies, from time to time, to the elements you take in too. Interviewers and counsellors need to overhaul/review their approach, repertoire of skills, and themselves, quite regularly.

Egan's 1986 version of his model is discussed here in this spirit. First, I will sketch my own present use of it. When counselling, I generally think in terms of three of his nine steps. I find more than this too complicated to be useful, although I am beginning to try thinking in terms of some of the other steps when reviewing a session or work with a particular client. I use the following three steps when counselling: Exploration, New Perspectives and Action. This is not an eccentric selection! It is consistent, broadly, with other interpretations of Egan's first (1975) version of his model, e.g. Inskipp and Johns (1983; 1984; 1985), Reddy (1987) and with Munro *et al.* (1983) and others.

Essentially, in stage one (I think of them as stages rather than steps), the counsellor seeks to communicate the core qualities with supporting skills. Staying in the client's frame of reference in this way is hard to do well, but it helps the client clarify, and contributes to forming a trusting relationship. There is a sense in which supporting skills also challenge; being listened to can be challenging, but it is in a different sense from stage two challenging, which comes from the counsellor's frame of reference. Stage one is sufficient for some clients. Change of attitude, or a decision about what to do, emerge naturally, without further help.

Stage two is, if necessary, offering new perspectives to the client, i.e. using challenge plus support, as described on p. 45. The client may then see his or her problem differently, 'reframe' it, feel differently about it. Action may then emerge without further help. Stage three – again if necessary – is helping the client decide what to do, and to evaluate the results.

The model is a guide, not a mechanical procedure, and some problems need only some of the stages or steps. Thus, some clients present one problem clearly, others many confused problems at once. Some need only stage one (or, more rarely, only a later stage), or stage one for one problem, but all three stages for another, and so on. It is flexible for style of counselling too. Thus Egan has become increasingly behavioural, with the current (1986) version emphasising goals and strategies more than earlier versions, but each counsellor can give the model their own emphasis and flavour. In general terms, the main value of the model remains: it *slows down* the way we normally respond to problems, with the aim of being more effective and saving time overall.

Either version of Egan's model of counselling or 'problem management' also provides a map and a framework. The map allows the counsellor to locate a particular point in the session or the purpose of a particular intervention, with implications for what to do next. The framework can also organise counselling techniques from other approaches, turning a haphazard eclecticism into a systematic one.

The 1986 model

The model is in three broad stages: helping the client (a) define and clarify a problem, (b) develop goals, and (c) take action. It is thus impeccably logical – indeed obvious – but not widely used. Instead, people tend for instance to think about actions before exploring their problem sufficiently or just to feel stuck and hopeless.

In *stage one* the counsellor uses the supporting and challenging skills discussed in the last section, taking care to 'earn the right' to challenge. However, the aim of stage one is more to help the client explore than to gather information. In terms of skills, this shift of emphasis means, crudely, paraphrase more and ask questions even less. Information may well be gathered very efficiently as a result but that is not the primary focus. First, the counsellor helps the client to 'tell their story', using supporting skills to see the story from the client's point of view. Then one problem or aspect of a problem is focused on, perhaps using one of Gilmore's techniques (p. 44). The counsellor also looks out for the strengths and resources of the client. If necessary, new perspectives are then offered, using both challenging and supporting skills.

A successful stage one (1986 version) results in a trusting relationship and a clear picture of the 'present scenario'. *Stage two* is the creation – in the client's imagination – of a *'new'* scenario'. What would the client's situation look like if it improved? Thus the client is asked to imagine a 'new scenario' with the counsellor asking questions like: 'What would be happening that is not happening now?' and 'What would you be doing differently from now?'

Egan (1986) sees counselling as a process for change more than for exploration; he emphasises the future 'rather than a past that cannot be changed or a present that is too problematic' (p. 277). Therefore the overall aim of stage two is to help the client set workable goals. Having created a new scenario, counsellor and client examine it. What might its consequences be, for the client and others, short-term and longer-term? Then the client chooses one or more goals. Concreteness, paraphrasing and the other supporting skills are highly relevant. The characteristics of workable goals include being specific, realistic, and consistent with the client's values.

Stage three is concerned with strategies for achieving the goals. Because the first strategy that comes to mind is not necessarily the best, the counsellor may encourage the client to 'brainstorm', i.e. to generate as many ideas as they can, however fantastic or silly. The next step, of course, is to clarify and evaluate the ideas, including ideas which may be concealed in bizarre possibilities, and then to try them out. In both action and goal-setting, taking *small steps* is a key principle. Again, supporting and challenging skills are used throughout.

The notion of small steps is related to another issue: how much change is possible? People *do* change – they become more assertive, more depressed, etc. – but a concept like 'basic character' clearly implies limits in important respects. Smail (1987) suggests that counselling is 'much less help than almost any of us can bear to think', but that this is *desirable*: we are not computers to be re-programmed. Similarly, Zilbergeld (1983) argues that we tend to hear only the dramatic success stories from counsellors and clients – and biased versions at that; that more often problems are reduced in intensity rather than 'cured'; that in any case many problems, e.g. depression, are best understood as normal human variation, and that recognising these limits can liberate a person to put energy into other things – 'I'm never going to be an X but what I can do well, and improve, is Y.' Whether Smail, Zilbergeld and the trait approach to counselling (Costa and McCrae, 1986) are right or not, the principle of taking small steps is a valuable one throughout Egan's model.

Egan (1986) breaks down the three stages more formally than I have done, and discusses each of nine steps at length. The steps provide a summary: stage one is (a) helping clients tell their story, (b) focusing and (c) challenging. Stage two is helping clients (a) construct a new scenario and set goals, (b) evaluate the goals, and (c) choose which goals to act on. Stage three is helping clients (a) develop strategies for action, (b) choose strategies, and (c) implement them.

Assertiveness

Assertiveness can be defined as 'expressing and acting on your rights as a person, while respecting the rights of other people'. It is included in this chapter because being more assertive in some respect is a common goal in counselling/ problem management, because assertive skills are themselves part of interviewing and counselling, most obviously in 'immediacy' but also in controlling the shape and process of an interview, and because of its relevance to support groups (p. 56).

Assertive skills include saying no, making requests and giving compliments. Like interviewing and counselling, assertiveness is not just about techniques; it thrives on accurate self-awareness and adequate self-esteem. If you know what you like and dislike, for example, it is easier to say no assertively. In this section, I will analyse the assertive skill of making requests, suggesting a sequence of steps which applies to using all the assertive skills. I choose making requests because of its contrast to the skill of paraphrasing: it is putting yourself to the fore rather than trying to see from another's point of view. In everyday life the two skills are complementary. Rogers (1975), at the level of personal qualities, argues for more empathy in relationships generally, but in everyday life for genuineness above all, i.e. stating your wants, intentions, feelings.

In analysing 'making requests', I will first note arguments for and against using the skill, second outline the basic skill – again in the form of suggestions to try out –

and third suggest refinements and subtleties. Two further skills – giving compliments and receiving compliments – are treated in the same way in Bayne (1989). Dickson (1987) is in my view the best practical book on assertiveness, for both sexes.

Arguments for and against making requests.   What stops people asking for something when they know what they would like? The reasons include:

—putting others first, 'It's not that important'.

—fear of rejection.

—not wanting to impose. One or both of you might be embarassed.

—Expecting people, especially if they care for you, to know without being asked. 'I shouldn't have to ask.' (I think of this as expecting telepathy.)

—Not wanting to be in debt to the other person.

On the other hand, there are consequences of *not* making requests:

—Frustration. Small irritations may build up until you 'explode' or you may express your frustration indirectly, e.g. by nagging, sulking, complaining to others, being a 'martyr'.

—You may lose touch with what you do want.

The general choice everyone makes is whether the results of not asking are worse or better for them than those of asking and being refused.

The basic skill

(1) Choose person and request carefully. (Remember the principle of small steps, here applicable to first attempts with a particular skill.)

(2) Write out the request; make sure it is brief, specific (concrete), and does not sabotage itself by implying either that they must agree or that you expect them to say no. Try to assume that you do not know their answer. (You are not telepathic either!) The request can be either for someone to do something, e.g. go for a drink, or to stop doing something, e.g. playing music too loudly for you.

(3) Rehearse (real or imaginary).
(4) Review the refinements below and consider their relevance to this request. Include them if they are relevant.
(5) Practise again. Observe in particular *how* you ask. Slight adjustments to the way you stand, hold your shoulders, or expression, will make you look, and probably feel, more assertive.
(6) Select time and place to actually make the request.
(7) Try it.
(8) Consider the outcome, using the principles of giving feedback (p. 33).

Refinements. When asking someone to stop doing something, or to do something they do not want to do, *calm repetition* can be a key element. The request tends to become easier to say as you repeat it, and to be said more definitely, as long as it is what you genuinely want. Repetition is also a way (perhaps combined with paraphrasing) of responding to protests and irrelevant logic. There is a superb example in Dickson (1987, p. 27) of such a conversation. Essentially, the idea is to say 'Yes I can see you are hurt/busy, etc. but I would like . . .', and so on. Second, you may like to suggest consequences (perhaps best held in reserve), or to combine your request with a compliment, itself an assertive skill and therefore with risks and benefits to be taken into account.

Psychological self-care

Anyone whose work involves counselling should – as a professional responsibility – take care of themselves too, both physically and psychologically (Nichols, 1988; Bond, 1986; Murgatroyd, 1985; British Association for Counselling (BAC) Code of Ethics, 1985). Strategies for psychological self-care tend also to be approaches to increasing self-awareness, at least in part – and self-awareness seems to be an essential part of good counselling. The argument for a high level of self-awareness is that only someone who knows themselves can listen and empathise. In its pure form this is over-stated: some 'blind spots' only prevent a counsellor being effective in a particular limited area. However, it does seem to be desirable for counsellors to both work on, and care for, themselves.

Self-awareness is used above in the relatively straightforward sense of 'awareness of inner experiencing', i.e. of thoughts, feelings, sensations, intuitions, fantasies, values. Becoming more self-aware in this sense is a matter of listening to oneself, of directing attention inwards. Many ingenious ways of doing this have been devised, e.g. Interpersonal Process Recall (Kagan, 1984) and the 'awareness wheel' (Inskipp and Johns, 1985). This section outlines two approaches to psychological self-care (and to increasing self-awareness): writing a journal and being in a support group. Three other approaches are discussed elsewhere in this book: assertiveness (p. 51), psychological type (p. 104), and relaxation (p. 34). Further possibilities include self-challenging of irrational beliefs (Murgatroyd, 1985), co-counselling (Murgatroyd, 1985; Evison and Horobin, 1984) and, of course, supervision or consultation.

Writing a journal is emphasised here because it is at once an approach to self-care and self-awareness and a method of practising counselling skills and qualities. A basic and quite structured method is described (cf. the approaches to journals of Progoff, 1975 and Rainer, 1980). It asks you to take your inner experience seriously, but guards against becoming morbidly introspective or unduly passive by emphasising action too, much as Egan's model does. A 'worked' example of the method is given, with comments. A different example, more directly related to work, is in Rayne (1989).

Writing a journal

Basic method

(1) Choose an experience that matters to you, e.g. part of a conversation, interview or counselling session, or something you've seen, done or read.

(2) Describe the experience in a sentence or two, or list key words. See if you can 'go into' and, to some extent, relive the experience.

(3) *Reflect on* your experience. Write as freely as you can – not analysing, not concerned with literary merit!

(4) *Analyse* your reactions and perhaps challenge them. Be specific.
What is the evidence for any asssertions, beliefs?
Is there a familiar feeling or pattern there?
What assumptions are you making?
Do your reactions tell you anything about yourself, e.g. suggest important values?
How realistic are you being?
What other ways (however unlikely) are there of looking at what happened?

(5) Consider *action*.
   (a) Is there any action you want to take now?
   (b) Is there anything which you might do differently next time?

If either (a) or (b) applies, plan (small steps) and perhaps rehearse.

'Worked' example

Wed.
Longer run than usual on Monday. In the night pain in my knee woke me up, and yesterday it was stiff and I hobbled. (*Steps 1 & 2*).
Felt despairing and angry: I'll have to stop running. Also annoyed that I'd just bought new running shoes, and disturbed by the strength of my reaction. I was flat and ill most of the day at work, and abrupt with some of my colleagues. During the day my knee eased. This morning it's near normal. Feel much more buoyant and constructive. I'm not crippled! (*End Step 3* – reflection – at least on this occasion).

I'm left wondering about my reaction to injury (and illness).
1) It's a recurring pattern. It may be related to lots of illness as a child, especially being scared I'd stop breathing.

2) Everyone is ill or injured sometimes (especially good athletes!). It's normal. (*End of Step 4* – a more considered analysis. Step 3 is written more freely, indeed as freely as possible).

Possible actions:
1) Look up knee injuries. Preventive measures?
2) Ask Dave's advice.
3) Make a special effort re 'flatness' next time: perhaps explain to other people, 'go into' my feelings, treat like *loss*. Do 1 and 2 today. (*End of Step 5* – possible actions).

Comment on the example. The steps overlap but the distinctions give some shape and sense of direction. Walker's (1985) advice to 'record less' (Step 2) and 'reflect more' (Step 3) has been followed, i.e. little emphasis on describing the event, more on reactions. Feelings are expressed. Analysis has been relatively neglected. The actions are feasible, but could be expressed more specifically.

Support groups

A support group usually consists of people in the same general situation who agree to offer support and challenge to each other. Dickson (1987, Chapter 3) gives some practical guidelines for self-help assertiveness groups and Bond (1986, Chapter 6) for support groups. The skills outlined earlier in this chapter are useful, in particular negotiating a contract, paraphrasing, and stating 'wants' and feelings. If an overall aim and strategy are agreed, then anything that happens in the group can be evaluated on whether it is consistent with the aims/strategy or not, e.g. the amount of time any one person in the group speaks, whether to allow silent members or not, to practise new behaviours or not, when to allow new members, and so on. One way of using the journal is to share extracts with another person, a 'supervisor' or a support group.

Conclusion

Interviewing, counselling and being assertive thrive on accurate self-awareness. They are not just skills but require work on yourself. Seeking and offering support, plus taping interviews, analysing them, training with others, etc. is a lot of work, justified because in Goffman's words (1968), there is 'no agent more effective than another person in bringing a world for oneself alive, or by a glance, a gesture or a remark, shrivelling up the reality in which one is lodged'.

Appendix 1: some difficulties and strategies

In this section some difficulties facing interviewers and counsellors, and possible strategies for dealing with them, are listed. You may find it most helpful to sample these now and return to them after particular interviews and with a completed checklist (Appendix 2). Many of the strategies are derived from the model and skills discussed in the rest of the chapter. Egan (1986) is a good general reference. The difficulties are divided into those with the process of interviewing and counselling; particular ways in which clients behave; and 'kinds' of client. 'General purpose' strategies are to paraphrase, to use 'immediacy' and to re-consider the contract.

A   Interviewing and counselling: process

Beginning.   See discussion of negotiating a contract (p 36). Give client a chance to compose themselves, get used to the room/you.

Ending.   Say 'In the last few minutes I'd like to . . .' or, nearer to the end, 'Is there anything else you want to say to me?' Try a summary, or ask the client to summarise. It is a good idea if possible to have some time to spare between interviews, both to prepare for the next one and because some clients leave important information until near the end. A contract helps. Try to end positively (not the same as false optimism): often there will have been some progress in understanding (Stage one p. 49), or some agreed action (Stage three p. 50). If verbal signals fail, try non-verbal: sit more upright and as a last resort stand up.

Note-taking.   Most people forget very quickly, roughly half of what is heard within a few hours of hearing it. Done skilfully, note-taking need not interfere with the pace and flow of the interview, and need not become more important than listening to the client. Against this, summaries help (by definition) to remember the relevant parts, and notes can be made immediately after the interview. Compromises are possible, e.g. not taking notes when the client is talking personally. Obviously, note-taking should not intrude. Clients can take notes too, or write out/draw aspects of a problem.

Embarrassing questions.   Introduce them. 'Some people find this an embarrassing question . . .'

B   Client behaviour

Too talkative.   Try summaries and a higher proportion of closed questions. Or remind the client of the contract, particularly of time. Interrupt. Say 'Can we return to . . .?'

Too quiet.   If open questions don't work, try closed ones. Attend more. Resist the temptation to talk too much yourself. Try paper and pencil techniques. You can ask 'Is there anything else you'd like to talk about?' or 'Would it help to sit and think about this for a while?'. (See also discussion of silence on p. 43.)

Nervous   Ask easy questions. Try to keep relaxed yourself, e.g. through breathing slowly and deeply.

Aggressive.   Try to avoid being trapped. If you are attacked, discuss it with colleagues, ask for support. (See Davies,

1988; Breakwell, 1989.) Aggressive people may be frightened. In any case threats are not likely to be useful: telling someone off probably tends to heighten aggression. Try using the person's name, paraphrase, especially to recognise their anger (see p. 39). Overall, show you are trying calmly to understand and want to help. Use assertiveness, e.g. 'I'd like you to stop shouting', 'I'd like to discuss the problem with you'.

Dishonest. Try prevention, e.g. such statements, made matter of factly, as, 'I know that you have two convictions for . . .'. Confrontation – rejecting the lie but not the client – may be preferable to a false relationship.

Drunk etc. Quiet words and actions. Offer help: what do *they* want to do? See notes under 'aggressive' above.

C *'Types of client'*

Bereaved. Recently bereaved people often feel lost and frightened. They may feel guilty about their behaviour towards the dead person, or angry with them for dying: whatever the feelings, pity is not appropriate and patience is. Our culture provides little preparation for death and interviewers too can find the subject difficult: it may stimulate a memory or a fear of loss in themselves. (See also p. 120 here, and Smith, 1982.)

In a crisis. 'Crisis' can apply to bereavement, illness, loss of job etc. Keep calm and still. Let the client cry, be quite, or talk, as they wish. This is emotional first aid: the person is not available for counselling. Counselling may be appropriate later. Encourage, support, give information to 'legitimise' the crisis. Ask about support from others. Suggest alternative actions, breaking down the immediate problem into manageable parts (Murgatroyd and Woolfe, 1982; see also Nelson-Jones, 1988, pp. 144–7; Castleman, 1988, Chapter 7; and Hopson 1981b, on a general model of loss).

Clients you dislike. Consider the opportunity for increasing your self-awareness!, i.e. you may discover or confirm a prejudice, e.g. against race, age, certain accents, characteristics associated with a significant person in your past etc. (An irrationally positive reaction is a prejudice too.) On the other hand, you may not be prejudiced against a particular client: he or she may actually be awkward, dogmatic, self-pitying, and you may feel less competent and helpful as a result.

Clients you are unable or unwilling to help.   Some problems are not soluble, others are not appropriate for you to deal with. So another skill is referral: when to refer (and feel positive about doing so), where and how. Mention the possibility of referral early, help the client to 'manage' (in Egan's sense) any doubts or worries etc.

Appendix 2: checklist for analysing your interviews/ counselling sessions

Please consider the aspects of your behaviour listed on this sheet, and where appropriate note examples. Remember the comments about developing skills (p. 33) and the notion of small steps.

Preparation

Did I:

Plan the interview? (e.g. decide about aim(s), structure). Prepare the seating etc.? Clear my mind?

Opening

Did I:

Welcome the client? Introduce myself? If necessary, attempt to put the client at ease?

Negotiate a contract and set boundaries?
Use basic listening skills?

Gathering information/Stage one of Egan's (1986) model

Did I:

Help the client say all he or she wanted to?
Help the client talk both freely and to the point?
Follow up leads?
Give the client the chance to explore feelings further?
Check understanding?
Help the client to focus?
Challenge (with support) when appropriate?
Other comments?

Stage two

Did I help the client:

Set workable goals?
Examine the consequences of achieving the goals?
Choose which goals to pursue?

Stage three

Did I help the client:

Generate a variety of strategies?
Evaluate the strategies (same criteria as for goals)?
Decide on action(s)?

Closing

Did I:

Agree a next step with the client?
End skilfully?

Overall

What state is the client in now compared with at the beginning?
What about my style, e.g. warm, abrasive, obscure, formal?
Any 'favourite' skills?
Favourite stages?
What about pace?
Mannerisms?
Posture?

Did I communicate:

Respect?
Empathy?
Genuineness?
What of value did the interview achieve?

Other comments?

Note that the checklist is a mixture of intentions and ways of trying to succeed in them. Your response to the checklist might combine evaluations – 'Yes, I did welcome the client well' – and comments on behaviour/skills – 'I used the client's name, I smiled (rather than beamed). I reflected the word 'better' in her first sentence well, but forgot to agree to a time in the 'contract' . . .' Then in your next interview, try to improve *one or two* aspects of your skills.

4

Groupwork Skills

Introduction

Individuals do not develop their personalities, relationships and ways of coping with the world in isolation. From the moment of birth infants are faced with the need to form relationships with their parents, who will be the means of providing the warmth, comfort and food essential for survival. Shortly afterwards children's experience commonly includes more than one adult, and often other children. Subsequently they will progress to relationships in the nursery, the school, friends near their home, all of which will provide them with a means of establishing patterns of behaviour, gaining an identity and learning a variety of roles.

So from the beginning we are faced with being members of a group, and as we grow older, the number of groups which are important to us and in which we are important, increases. Social workers need to recognise that their clients have a history of belonging to, and being influenced by, a variety of social types of behaviour (for instance, truanting behaviour in teenagers may be the result of peer group pressure. It may be easier for a child to miss school, and risk the consequences, than go against the other members of their peer group). The social worker must also understand the dynamics (i.e. interactions) in, for example, a family or a children's home, in order to intervene effectively. An appreciation of group psychology not only helps with understanding and assessing a client's situation, but also enables social workers to utilise group forces in a therapeutic way.

63

This chapter aims to summarise the psychological theory of group dynamics (which is referred to again in Chapter 7, when considering relationships within social work settings) and gives a guide to groupwork skills which make use of such theory. The chapter begins by defining the term 'group' and examines examples of the type of study which has contributed to an understanding of group behaviour. Then it looks at the influence groups have upon individual members, followed by the theory concerned with the development and changes in the structure of the group itself (group dynamics). The last part of the chapter looks at why and how social workers might set up a group, and the skills necessary for conducting group sessions.

Definition of the term 'group'

A group can be defined in a number of ways, which relate to its function, the nature of its membership (i.e. why people join and whether membership is voluntary) and its goals and eventual purpose. In this book it seems appropriate to consider a definition of the 'group' in its widest context, as follows:

> A group is an aggregate of individuals standing in certain descriptive (i.e. observable) relations to each other. The kinds of relations exemplified will of course depend on or determine the kind of group whether it is a family, or an audience, a committee, union, or crowd. (Cartwright and Zander, 1968)

From this definition it becomes clear that there are several kinds of group. It is worth noting this before moving on to consider what is important in the field of group dynamics. Groups can be divided into two categories:

The primary group is a group in which members come face-to-face, regardless of any other characteristics. These groups can be natural groups such as the family, or a group of friends, or they can be formal, like a school class, or a therapeutic group. It is the primary group which is central to this chapter.

Secondary groups are slightly more difficult to identify, but just as important because even though they do not necessarily come face-to-face, the potential members have characteristics in common. For instance, they may be single parent families, the parents of children who go to a particular school, or old people isolated in their homes. (See Twelvetrees, 1982, for a discussion of secondary groups in the community.)

The study of group behaviour

The first attempt at an analysis of group behaviour was made at the end of the last century by a Frenchman called Le Bon, whose book *The Crowd* illustrated his observation that individuals in a large group show behaviour that does not constitute the total of their behaviour as individuals. This means that there appears to be some feature of this large group which cannot be traced to individual members. He considered that some sort of 'collective mind' emerges and that in addition, forces of contagion and suggestibility are at work, and the group acts as if it is hypnotised. In *Group Psychology and The Analysis of the Ego* (1922), Freud evaluated Le Bon's work against psychodynamic theory, and argued that the binding force of the group derives from the emotional ties of the members, which are expressions of their libido.

In the USA during the 1930s, social psychologists began to study group dynamics systematically. Kurt Lewin, one of the early researchers, became a very important name in this field. He established the Research Center for Group Dynamics at the Massachusetts Institute of Technology, and the National Training Laboratories in Bethel, Maine. In Britain, psychologists and some psychiatrists became interested in studying groups during the 1940s. The work of Bion, Maine, Jones and others at the Tavistock Institute led to innovations in group psychotherapy, and the study of organisations incorporating psychoanalytic theory.

Other social scientists have made important studies of group behaviour, and it is useful here to distinguish briefly between the particular perspectives from which other disciplines have approached this subject. Sociologists have concentrated on studying natural groups such as the family, work groups, the military prisons, hospitals, and are concerned with the function and meaning of the social institutions they study. So, for instance, they try to make useful statements about the functions of the family, or the meaning of the family in western capitalist society. Anthropologists have generally employed the technique of participant observation and looked at the way groups live in particular societies. They are more concerned with how people establish their norms and value systems, and the different cultures that emerge. For instance, they might be able to show the significance of the event of childbirth in a society, and the consequent roles and rituals that emerge.

There are four main perspectives employed by psychologists:

(1) They are interested in the way groups influence the behaviour, personality, social development, and attitudes of the individuals within them, i.e. the effects of the group on the individual member.
(2) They are interested in the characteristics of the groups themselves: how they form, change, develop norms, how they are structured. This kind of study is the one most frequently referred to as the study of *group dynamics*.
(3) Deriving from the study of group dynamics and the effect of group pressure on individuals, emerge studies relating to the effectiveness of particular groups. These studies have been part of applied psychology, and are particularly relevant to education, training and therapy, although they also have applications to less palatable activities such as running prison camps, and torture.
(4) There have also been investigations of intergroup co-operation and conflict, with obvious implications for political activity – alliances, warfare, dealing with terrorist activity, hijackers, sieges, and so on.

The individual in the group: social influence

Social influence is the phrase used by psychologists to

describe the pressure for *similarity* which is active in all societies. This pressure affects and changes behaviour and attitudes in the direction of prevailing patterns in a particular culture or sub-culture. Although outstanding and unusual people are highly esteemed and a certain admiration is usually afforded to originality, on the whole society values those who share its collective culture and adhere to its rules.

There are three major forms of influence:

Uniformity – which is the similarity which rests on an individual's acceptance of the unspoken assumption that being like others is desirable.
Conformity – which is the similarity that develops when an individual gives in to social pressure to be like others.
Obedience – which is the similarity that rests on compliance with the demands of an authority figure.

There is a great deal of social influence at work within social work teams, which is discussed in Chapter 7. And most people who become social workers' clients are at the mercy of pressures which either cause or emphasise their difficulties. An example is the influence of the peer group on adolescents, which might cause them to deviate from the rules of wider society. Similarly, a father who is out of work, and unable to fulfil the role that his family expect (be like other fathers – be the breadwinner, be dominant, and so on) might see himself as inadequate, his relationships might deteriorate and his emotional health might reach a critical stage.

Psychologists have investigated which particular factors are most important in influencing people towards uniformity, conformity and obedience. The importance of *social norms* in all three · areas is clearly demonstrated. Social norms represent the expectations of all members of a society or group. They can be about what is acceptable behaviour in particular circumstances, or about attitudes group members may hold, or about what 'qualifications' members are expected to have achieved. In other words they are rules which represent values which group members consider important, and are thus incorporated into the culture of the society or group.

Social norms may be internally or externally derived. Internal norms are the ones which are particularly relevant to behaviour during social interaction, and are consequently of most concern to psychologists. External norms are those which members bring to the group from their lives outside its influence. Social psychologists have made many studies of normative behaviour; some of these have taken place in a laboratory setting, and others in day-to-day living. For example, Garfinkel's (1967) study showed the importance of social norms for people's expectations about each others' behaviour. He hypothesised that there are many unseen rules which govern our behaviour, which we only discover when they are broken, leading to subsequent punishment. He told his students to test these hidden rules in their homes, by acting as 'paying guests' for a period of fifteen minutes. They were to be polite, respectful, and suitably distant towards their families, and only to speak when spoken to. The next day, the students' reports were filled with accounts of their parents' anxiety, astonishment, embarrassment and anger. They had been accused of selfishness and moodiness, and considering this experiment had only lasted for fifteen minutes, and did not constitute openly hostile behaviour, it is an illustration of just how powerful these norms actually are.

One of the classical social psychology experiments was carried out by Sherif in the 1930, and concerned the auto–kinetic effect. This is an optical illusion in which a stationary pinpoint of light viewed in an otherwise dark room appears to be moving. Sherif placed a great many subjects in a darkened room and allowed them to make independent assessments about how far the light had moved. He then brought groups of subjeccts together and asked them to repeat the task. The group's judgements *converged* on a central estimate of motion, and even when Sherif tested them later he found that group consensus persisted. Thus a social norm was established, and endured despite its lack of authentic foundation.

Studies of the pressure towards uniformity have indicated that the phenomenon of *modelling* is also important. This is copying the behaviour of an influential person, or model, such as a parent, group leader, or pop singer. (See Chapter 6 for more details in relation to social learing theory, p. 115). Also, people often judge themselves by seeing how much they agree with other people. This is called social comparison, and contributes towards uniformity. Finally, uniformity is also brought about by the desire to avoid feeling odd or standing out from the crowd. Psychologists have called this objective self-awareness, but it is better described in daily use as self-consciousness.

Conformity may be understood in three ways: first, in terms of *compliance*, when people conform in their behaviour but do not necessarily alter their attitudes. Motives for compliance are often connected with survival, or status and security. An example would be a prisoner who changes his behaviour in order to conform to the rules of the institution (or even to the inmate sub-culture) but inwardly does not alter original hostile feelings. Cohen and Taylor's (1972) study of long-term prisoners showed several examples of this, and a classic psychological study was undertaken by Asch in a series of experiments in the 1950s. This involved a subject having to say which of three comparison lines was equal in length to a standard line, when all four lines were simultaneously presented. When the subject tackled the task alone there was a high degree of accuracy. However, the naïve subjects were then placed in the midst of a group of the experimenter's confederates, who always chose the wrong line deliberately. Asch found that one third of the time the naïve subject agreed with the wrong answer in this situation.

This work demonstrated that individuals are greatly influenced by the pressure towards conformity, even when they probably realise that the group consensus does not provide the correct solution. However, the results of this study have been criticised by other psychologists, who stress that the results should not be generalised: if there was always such pressure to outward compliance then new ideas would never be established, and individual innovations would never get accepted. it has also been found that committed *minorities* in groups can persuade other group members to their point of view, and compliance is thus related to more than majority pressure.

Secondly, *identification* occurs when one person finds it important to be like another. This is referred to as classical identification. Sometimes it is important for someone to meet the *expectations* of another person. This is called reciprocal-role identification, and happens a great deal in marriages or between bosses and secretaries, or social workers and clients. Thirdly, a person might be happily influenced by another if she/he finds the behaviour and attitudes of that person consistent with his/her own values. This is called *internalisation*. The influence of a religious leader is a good example of this.

Interest in obedience increased after the trials of the Nazi war criminals, who claimed that they had committed atrocities as a result of obeying orders, and felt that they should not be held individually responsible for their actions. Stanley Milgram performed a series of what are now famous studies to discover just how far people in general will go when ordered to do something. Theses are described in his book *Obedience to Authority* (1974). He set up a laboratory where naïve subjects were told that they were assisting in an experiment to assess the effects of punishment on learning. The subject was told that the learner, to whom he was introduced, would be in the next room, wired up to a machine which would administer a shock every time the subject pressed a button. The subject was shown a dial which would increase the shock from light to dangerous, and the experimenter told him that he should increase this each time a wrong answer was given. A battery was temporarily attached to a lead, and the subject was given a mild shock just to prove the machine worked. In fact this was the only shock to be administered, as the machine was a fake! Before running his experiments, Milgram sought the views of several psychologists and psychiatrists who said that it would be very unlikely that his subjects would continue the experiment after the first couple of shocks.

During the experiment the subjects asked the 'learner' certain questions, and when a wrong answer was given, the experimenter told the subject to press the shock button.

After a few times the 'learner' started begging the subject to stop, and the experimenter told the subject to go on, despite the subject's protests. The 'learner' claimed that he had a weak heart, and when the final 'shock' was administered, the screaming stopped, and there was silence. The conditions were varied. Sometimes there was a window so that the subject could see the learner's reactions, at some times the experimenter appeared scruffy and inconsequential, at others well dressed and authoritative. Milgram thought that these factors might affect the degree of obedience. On average, about 62 per cent of subjects obeyed the experimenter until told they might stop, and about one third proceeded until the learner was silent. Some of the subjects expressed great anguish both during the experiments and for some time afterwards, but this was not enough to stop them, and it seems that many people will do as they are told under particular circumstances even though they regret doing it.

Group dynamics

Social groups which exert influence over their members are not themselves uniform in nature, but are constantly changing as a result of the influence of individual members and external demands.

Group structure

Once a group has formed, a structural pattern begins to develop, and the role, interpersonal preference, communication, status and power structures emerge, along with patterns of normative behaviour. The developments and changes in these structures are referred to as group processes or group dynamics. The structure of a group may or may not be affected by formal organisations, but even if it is, informal group structures can be observed. So a team within the probation service has its formal structural relationships dictated by the Assistant Chief Probation

Officer, i.e. that the Senior Probation Officer is in charge of the office and makes the major decisions, but informally the Senior Probation Officer may frequently and deliberately enlist the skills of basic grade colleagues in a variety of important tasks.

Groups come together formally or informally in order to perform certain tasks, to be carried out as well as they are able. Groups in which all the members wish to be part, which agree on the tasks to be performed, and recognise the members who are most suitable for each role, are likely to be the most effective. All groups aim at close proximity to this state, but it can rarely be achieved without conflict, and it is this conflict which causes groups to develop and change their structure. A group which is concentrating upon personality or behavioural change in its members might be encouraging everyone to share their fears, anxieties and intimate details of their past lives. If some members do not reveal things in this way, others will feel frustrated and betrayed, and the group will not represent a 'safe' environment for change. The pressure aimed at the 'non-disclosing' members will be manifest in a struggle between the group and individual members about norms, criteria for membership, tasks and roles, and if all eventually agree and feel able to share their intimate feelings, then this is seen as a measure of effectiveness. The process by which the pressure is applied, the alliances which form and the changing patterns of communications, friendship and roles, are the dynamics of the group.

Ralph Linton (1949), one of the first social scientists to consider that a group was an entity, looked at group properties. He felt that these could be divided into structural (e.g. patterns of relationship among members) and dynamic (e.g. expressions of the changes in group relationships) properties; distinct from each other, but closely interwoven. Linton, and also Newcomb (1953), further analysed these properties in terms of status and role structure. The status structures were static, and referred to a collection of rights and duties attributed to the occupant of a particular position in a group. An individual is assigned to a status position and occupies it in relation to other statuses: someone who has been officially designated group leader because of their training in group psycho-therapy has a right to occupy this status, because other people are members, whose status requires them to recog-nise the leader's status! The leader also has a duty to use the knowledge and skills which she has, and which have led to their achieving that status. The role structure represents the dynamic aspects of the status position, whereby the occupant of the role puts the rights and duties of her status into effect, and performs the tasks relating to the role of leader/psychotherapist, as in this example.

Linton stresses that status and role are quite inseparable, and that there can be no roles without statuses, and no statuses without roles. Newcomb employed the concept of position rather than status, with the role being seen as the behaviour of people who occupy positions. Every position which is recognised by the members of a group contributes in some way to the purposes of the group, and this contribution represents the group function.

Types of group structure

The affect structure, or interpersonal preference structure, refers to the degree of attraction between group members, and is a powerful determinant of *group cohesiveness*. If attraction between group members is intense, then high value is placed on membership, and the group is said to be cohesive. This may be adversely affected by:

(1) an increased number of members, which might mean priority has to be established in power and control of activities, with a greater number of people in subordi-nate positions.
(2) the formation of sub-groups, or cliques by people who are particularly attracted to each other. This means that an intergroup rivalry will occur within the main group, which will reduce cohesiveness.

The affect structure can be diagramatically represented on a sociogram, a technique invented by Moreno (1934). See

Figure 1. The sociogram describes who likes whom, who is rejected by the group, who is the most popular, and where the cliques exist.

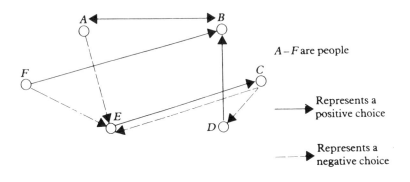

A – F are people

Represents a positive choice

Represents a negative choice

Figure 1   *An example of a sociogram*

Most groups are constrained by a communications structure which is imposed upon them. This might be that the area director cannot directly supervise the work of a basic grade social worker, and so she has to do this via the team leader/or it might be that a particular residential home has a policy that each worker and residents' views and opinions have to be considered publicly before decisions are taken. Psychologists have studied whether different communications structures hinder the development of group processes or assist in the performance of group tasks. It is apparent that communication structures fulfil different functions more efficiently. The important variable is often the degree of centralisation in a communication network structure, see Figure 2.

The wheel is the most centralised pattern, and the circle the least centralised. The wheel facilitates simple decision-making, but is bad for the morale of peripheral group members. For more complex tasks the circle pattern often proves superior. This may be because of more active participation by all members, which itself increases morale, or because in the wheel the centralised person may well be overlooked.

The *power structure* in a group relates to the roles and status positions of its members. There is also an additional

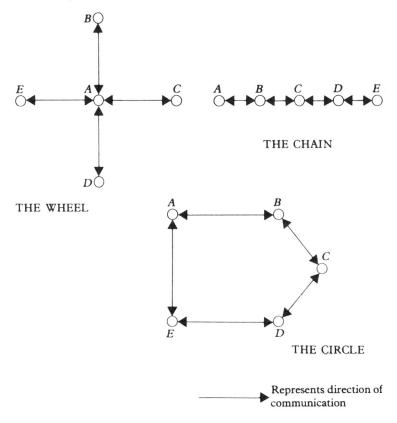

THE CHAIN

THE WHEEL

THE CIRCLE

Represents direction of communication

Figure 2 *Examples of some types of communication structures*

component which is related to the influence a member exerts over the others during social interaction. Social power has been defined as 'the potential influence of some influencing agent O, over some person, P. Influence is defined as a change in cognition, attitude, behaviour or emotion of P which can be attributed to O' (French and Raven, 1959). There are different types of powers which can be based on the ability of a group member to reward, coerce, provide expert knowledge, provide information or have other members wishing to be like him/her, or having a legitimate reason for power. Different power is important at different times during the life of a group, and although the sources of power are not independent (one person may have influence through more than one source of power) it is likely that power shifts between members.

As described earlier, the *role structure* represents the dynamic aspects of the status positions. Certain groups have formal roles, such as mother, father, son, daughter, teacher, therapist, and so on, but all have informal role structures in addition. The most important of these are 'leader', 'follower', 'scapegoat', 'lieutenant' (second-in-command and support to the leader). Again, there are various ways in which these informal roles are occupied. For instance the leader may be permanent, short-term, a task leader, an emotional leader. The reason why certain individuals occupy particular roles varies according to the other aspects of structure, group task and personality.

Groupwork

The first part of this chapter has focused attention upon the information available to explain aspects of social behaviour, and reflects upon the importance of a *social existence*. It is important for groupwork leaders to be aware that group members are influenced by the social constraints which have been described, as well as by their own personality and individual histories. Superimposed upon the interaction of the individual group members is the action of group structure and group dynamics: the group itself can be understood independently of the effect its members have upon each other. The leader has to make sense of this aspect of group life in order to be useful to members seeking help and support.

Groupwork in many ways represents a break with traditional social work and its casework relationship between professional worker and client. It has grown in popularity in Britain since the 1960s, partly as a response to criticisms of traditional methods, and partly as a result of emerging as an established force in social work in the USA by 1960. The term 'groupwork' demands a more detailed definition and explanation, especially since within its broad framework there are a variety of models for practice deriving from a diverse body of theory, but at this stage groupwork may be described as 'social work in which one or more social workers is involved in professional practice with a group of probably more than four clients at the same time'. The aims and objectives and the shared characteristics of the members, and the tasks they perform, may vary greatly.

Despite an increase in popularity and a general acceptance of its validity as a method of social work, it is still true to say that groupwork in Britain is a peripheral activity in most fieldwork agencies. Many social work training courses only give it a brief acknowledgement (although this is not universally true), and it is generally seen as a method of 'prevention' rather than a serious way of dealing with social deprivation. Many agencies expect those of their staff with groupwork skills and commitment to develop groupwork activities as 'spare time extras', which reinforces this belief, even among social workers themselves. Residential and day-care institutions tend to value group activities more highly, due to the nature of their work. However, rarely is the work of these institutions seen to have as high a status as fieldwork. We hope this chapter will make a contribution towards persuading the reader of the potential of groupwork *generally* within social work practice.

A social worker should be aware of group influences upon individual clients, and also of changes in the structure of the formal (e.g. therapeutic) and informal (e.g. people in his office) groups with which he is involved. It is important for the social worker to realise that no member either starts or finishes her particular group experience solely as a member of one particular group. Even long-stay psychiatric patients and prisoners experience diverse effects and reactions to their circumstances, which reflect the influence of other groups to which they have belonged, currently identify with, and aspire to join in the future. Thus all people are influenced by the groups they have contact with, and either choose membership or drop out. In order to function at all, formal groups have to generate norms, even if they are constructed around simple issues such as the length of time group members have to remain together at each meeting. The more effective a group is to become, the more committed its members must be, and this in turn results in a more highly developed and complex set of group norms.

So, in order to sustain its membership, a group must reflect the needs of its members. The social worker setting up a group with highly specific aims and goals might find difficulty in directing the group towards these if the members themselves do not recognise them as their own. Groupwork goals should be flexible, and bear relationship to goals set by members, including the group leader. In order to do this successfully, the social worker has to maintain a grasp of:

● Group dynamics
● The skills needed to set up a group
● Running group meetings so that members are able to explore their own needs and the extent to which that group might meet them.

Groupwork is a generic term. There is no one theoretical or methodological approach which is all-embracing, and the only common feature is that a social worker will be involved in setting up, and probably running, the group: she may or may not be concerned with emotional or environmental change for the group members, and equally may or may not participate in group meetings. The intention of this section is to examine the groupwork skills appropriate to social work, and therefore the focus will be on social work intervention, rather than on group psychotherapy.

A frequently quoted and reasonably adequate definition of groupwork is offered by Konopka (1963). She says that 'Social groupwork is a method of social work which helps individuals to enhance their social functioning through purposeful group experiences, and to cope more effectively with their personal, group, or community problems.' This definition stresses the wide-ranging scope of the method, in that community problems can be dealt with as well as personal and group ones, but an emphasis remains upon the inadequacies of the group members, in that they need to 'cope more effectively' and have particular 'problems' in their lives. Groupwork may also be concerned with non-problem-centred groups such as 'support' and 'conscious-raising' groups. These provide a chance to explore wider implications of an individual's position in society, and highlight certain features of particular life-styles which can be destructive or inhibit growth and change. So for instance, a social workers' support group provides opportunities to explore the position of social workers in a bureaucratic system, the way their clients are treated as a result, and to gain help from, and give help to, their colleagues.

The scope of groupwork

There are many facets of activity which can be included within the term 'groupwork'. These may be divided into several related categories:

(1) The method employed by the workers, especially in terms of leadership style.
(2) The theoretical basis upon which the group is formed and conducted.
(3) The goals of the group according to the worker.
(4) The consumers of groupwork, and what they wish to achieve as members.
(5) The format of group events – whether they occur regularly, sporadically, are part of institutional life,

whether membership fluctuates, and the lifespan of the group, and the nature of group activity (i.e. it is primarily a 'talking' or practical group?)

Based on these components, several models of groupwork have emerged:

● Social groupwork
● Therapeutic groupwork or group therapy
● Community work
● Self-help and support groups

Within these models there is still opportunity to develop particular approaches. The models are probably distinguished by their focus on a particular section of the potential client population: social groupwork is frequently offered to clients who need to develop their social skills and experiences, such as isolated mothers, or teenagers who are having problems at home or at school; group therapy to people suffering from emotional or psychiatric problems who have identified their needs (or had them identified) as having to change some aspects of their behaviour or emotional reactions; community work usually focuses upon people who identify the root of their problem in terms of environmental deprivation or social injustice, and this model operates in order to help them clarify the issues and work together to effect social change. Consciousness-raising became more popular in the late 1960s and 1970s, with the acknowledgement that social oppression had greatly restricted the political, social and emotional life of certain social groups. The most obvious of these are racial minorities, women, and the handicapped, but also children, the working class, pensioners and other segments of society which have learned to recognise the external constraints on their lives and make efforts to understand and change them.

The self-help or support group model is perhaps the widest-ranging in terms of who might benefit. Many self-help groups have emerged, usually under social work leadership. Any group of people with mutual needs or problems may benefit from regular contact with others tackling similar problems. An example of this might be people wishing to set up a playgroup for their own community, a group of ex-alcoholics in Alcoholics Anonymous, or a group of social workers discussing professional concerns.

Embarking upon groupwork

Most statutory social work agencies put little pressure on their staff to undertake any groupwork, and it may well appear that they discourage it by giving casework overriding priority. There are several explanations for this. The basic one is probably that most social workers and social work mangers lack particular training in groupwork, and avoid the possibility of getting out of their depth. There are similarities in the aims and skills of all types of social work, but working with groups of clients can expose the social worker to a potentially threatening situation where she/he will be in the minority, and thus less 'powerful' than in other social work activities.

Additionally for several reasons groups are often best conducted by two social workers, and those groupworkers will be exposing their professional skills to scrutiny which rarely occurs first-hand outside the groupwork role. Although social workers report on their interactions with clients, and seek support from their senior staff, their interpersonal skills are rarely in question. Agencies evaluate social work according to the effectiveness of administration and action in connection with their clients' lives. Less emphasis is placed upon personal contact and interaction with clients once social workers get beyond their training, and even then, social worker/client contact is generally assessed by way of 'process recordings' or verbal accounts rather than personal observation by supervisors. Similarly, social workers rarely know the details of their colleagues' relationships with their clients, which provides difficulties for assessments of clients' needs in a team with respect to offering groupwork. However, there are several reasons why groupwork might be very acceptable to both clients and staff of statutory and voluntary agencies.

Advantages of groupwork

(1) Most people's lives involve situations where they are members of large and small groups. Their experiences result directly from their social position, and therefore it is often useful to confront their problems in a group setting. These are not necessarily emotional problems, but may involve difficulties in a variety of interpersonal settings, e.g. dealing with bureaucracies, people in authority, their own families, etc.

(2) All members of the group have certain resources which may well provide help and support for other members.

(3) Groups can be made up of people with similar problems and experiences who can provide reassurance, insight and support to each other, in the way professional workers cannot.

(4) For people who wish to change some part of their behaviour or personality, a group experience is much more likely to be effective than the traditional approach.

(5) The social worker is potentially less powerful in the group situation where the other members are always in a majority. Thus his behaviour and decisions are always open to challenge.

(6) Certain social worker/client relationships are traditionally unfruitful. For instance, adolescents on Supervision Orders often need help, but the prescribed statutory involvement requires the social worker to 'advise and befriend' and this is usually impossible. Problems may well be exacerbated by the imposed presence of an authority figure, but the adolescent may be able to confront and deal with them if they can be shared with others in a similar position.

(7) There is a likelihood that once groupwork is established in an agency, it will be economical in terms of social work time. Certainly some people will always require some individual contact, either in relation to statutory tasks, or simply because they need to relate to a professional worker, but these contacts could be kept to the minimum.

(8) Groupworkers have more chance to gain feedback on their professional ability both from clients and from their co-worker.

Disadvantages of groupwork

(1) If members of a group are really going to tackle important issues, they will not have the same guarantee of confidentiality as a one-to-one relationship with a social worker.
(2) A great deal of time and effort is involved in setting up and running a group, and often colleagues in an agency are not particularly supportive.
(3) It is necessary to have access to certain physical resources: accommodation, equipment, catering facilities, transport, care facilities for pre-school children.
(4) Sometimes, social workers find problems in running groups and may not be able to deal with certain 'explosive' situations which arise, which may be more intense because of the group context.
(5) Group membership and selection for membership inevitably results in 'labelling' of individuals as 'depressed mothers', 'school refusers' and so on. There may be a stigma attached to group membership because of this, as selection for membership depends upon individuals having some sort of identifiable 'problem'.
(6) Individual members might find that they are not getting as much from the group sessions as they would from a one-to-one session, possibly because one or two other members constantly compete for attention, or they discover that they do not share the same experiences or difficulties as most of the other members of the group.
(7) Particular individuals might experience rejection by the group which reflects their real life difficulties. The degree to which this may or may not be helpful depends on the commitment of the member and the skill of the groupworkers.

Deciding whether groupwork is appropriate

The decision to start a groupwork project is based upon three separate, but not mutually exclusive factors:

(1) The social workers concerned should be committed to groupwork as a form of intervention. This is not to suggest that they are not also committed to other forms of social work, but that they must be convinced of the validity of groupwork itself.
(2) There must be some means of identifying and acknowledging the needs of potential group members.
(3) Certain basic physical resources must be available.

Most people's experience of social work does not include groupwork, and so prospective group members should be made fully aware of exactly what is being offered.

Setting up the group

Groupwork needs careful preparation. Decisions have to be made which involve apparently endless permutations – the result being that a form of compromise has to be reached by the groupworkers as to:

● who the group members will be,
● the type of group they are going to run (e.g. a 'practical' group or a 'talking' group),
● the length and time of day for each session. Enough time must be available for 'ice-breaking' at each session, despite pressures that the members and workers will probably face concerning their commitments. One and a half to two hours is generally considered suitable. It is also important to take account of the daily routines of potential members, so that a group is not organised mid-afternoon for mothers who have to collect children from school, or an afternoon group for people who are at work.

● the frequency of the sessions and the duration of the life of the group. Many people may not favour a long-term commitment, but will be happy to meet as frequently as twice a week. For instance, a group for school children during the summer vacation may meet intensively for a relatively short period, enabling them to get to know each other quickly, and so gain the most from the experience. A community group wishing to confront specific problems in an area may wish to meet once a fortnight, as they may be dealing with separate tasks between meetings. It is often a good idea to set a limited number of sessions with the option for the group to review this in the light of experience and achievement at the end of that period.

Aims of the group

The considerations which arise during the planning stages of a group's life must also be taken into account when planning the group's aims. It is important for the group-workers to be clear about what they plan to achieve and how. These aims may be flexible, and should certainly be reviewed, preferably after each session. This does not mean, to take an extreme example, that a group for school refusers must constantly focus on the central topic; indeed it may well be that not going to school is *not* particularly important for the lives of the group members. It does mean that a group must set realistic aims which reflect the workers' intentions and abilities, and the members' needs. Being realistic would mean that a group for people attending a day centre for ex-psychiatric patients would not aim to get the members back into full-time employment in three months. It might however aim at enabling the members to take an active part in planning their daily routines, to learn to talk about themselves and their difficulties with each other, and listen to the problems of other members, and it is likely that the group experience would enable them to achieve these aims.

Selecting the group members

Referrals for groupwork may come from a variety of sources
which clearly depend upon the agency and type of group.
Groups which depend on a system of referral are usually
those run by statutory agencies, or those which cater for the
needs of a specific section of the population. Some will have
methods of self-selection, as in the case of a community-
based group, or there may be a method of group selection
as in some therapeutic communities. Some groups are non-
selective, and these would include 'drop-in' centres, play-
groups, and luncheon clubs. They do, however, tend to
attract people who identify in some way with the people
who regularly attend.

Apart from the referral and selection of members, it is
necessary to establish whether a group is to be 'open' or
'closed': whether or not new members should be able to
join, and others drop out at any stage. The decision about
this rests with the group leaders, and should be clarified
before potential members are recruited.

Groupwork in action

The processes and dynamics of each group depend on the
leadership and the members, but as we have seen earlier in
this chapter, there are also certain developmental sequences
which are common to all groups, regardless of the characteristics of members. These relate to group composition and
size, group cohesiveness, and conflicts which surround the
stated and unstated aims. They reflect the establishment of
rules and norms, the degree of commitment and attraction
of the members, and the way in which the group processes
are handled by the group workers. The leader should be
aware of the group processes, that is the development of the
group itself as distinct from the behaviour of the individuals
comprising it. Several groupwork writers have described the
stages of group development resulting from changes in the
structure which occur in response to the group needs at a
particular time. Tuckman (1965) has summarised the

sequence of events in group development as *forming*, *norming*, *storming* and *performing*, and subsequent writers have suggested a final stage of *mourning*. Groupworkers have a specific part to play at each stage of development, and recognising and understanding the stages will enable them to do this.

Forming. Initially group members will come together knowing very little about each other, and why they are there. They will probably have accepted the leader's explanation that they can share similar problems and experiences with others, but there will be all sorts of doubts and anxieties in their minds about who speaks to whom, when to speak, whether or not to launch into discussion of their problems immediately, or whether they want to disclose anything at all to this bunch of strangers they are now faced with! At this stage the groupworkers play an important part in the interaction. They decide the style of introductions, which set the tone of the first and subsequent meetings. For instance, the leaders might start by telling the group their names, a bit about their work, why they set up the group and what they are hoping it will achieve. They could then ask the members to do something similar.

In practically-oriented groups the workers may assign specific tasks to members, such as setting out chairs, making coffee, buying the provisions or checking the equipment, in order to establish individuals with a role. If the group is one in which members already know each other, as in a hospital or day centre, it is particularly important to stress the aims, functions and boundaries of the group, as distinct from the other activities which members might share. Groups in residential and day-care settings frequently do operate successfully, and most people are able to distinguish between their different roles in the group, and in other activities in the same setting.

Storming. Once the members have established who they are and why they are there, it often appears important for some people, or the group as a whole, to rebel against the leaders, or to question the aims and usefulness of the group.

It is also frequently true that they will not achieve their aims, or that their problems are insoluble. It is very much a reaction against the initial excitement and optimism on joining a group and meeting others with similar hopes and fears, and then realising that there is more to effective group membership than just sharing these. The group leader has to avoid feeling the same hopelessness, and possibly has to exert more control over individuals than she/he might at some later stage. This is a difficult balance to maintain because too much or too little control could prevent the group from actually becoming a cohesive, effective force in its own right. It is important that the leader questions these attacks and hopeless feelings posed by the members, but does *not* attack the individuals who raise the doubts. It is likely that one or several members will say that they do not feel that sitting in a room for two hours a week will help with their particular difficulties.

Group leaders at all stages, but particularly this one, should respond as much as possible by *opening up* the issues rather than providing a definitive answer. This can be done in a number of ways. For instance, in answer to a personal attack on the leader by a member it might be appropriate to answer by straightforward explanation or denial, but it is likely to be more useful to ask whether other members have seen the leader in the same way, and if the group replies that they have, then the leader might carry on to ask what the group feels she/he could do to make it feel more comfortable. If not the group might focus on why the deviant member feels as he does. Although many people may remain silent during confrontation, if the leader opens up the discussion, other people are frequently able to contribute, and either support or refute the attack. Subsequent discussion may prove fruitful for all involved enabling the group to resolve certain basic conflicts.

Similarly, if a member is 'going off at a tangent', or doing all the talking (often addressing themselves to the leaders rather than to the rest of the group), it is important to try and allow other members to control the discussion if possible. The leader could ask 'what do other people think?', or if this fails, something along the lines of 'It would seem as if Christine has a lot on her mind just now. I wonder if other people have had similar experiences . . .' or 'whether other people can suggest to her how to deal with . . .' If someone senses the group's lack of direction and is allowed to take over, other members may well feel that the group has no place for them, and their suspicions and anxieties will be confirmed. With appropriate 'facilitation' at this early stage, members should be able to deal with over-enthusiastic orators at a later stage of the group's development, preventing the need for too much leadership control over participation.

Norming. During the 'storming' stage, individuals are trying to establish their roles, and work out their values in relation to the rest of the group members. As members become more committed to the group and each other, they establish norms and as a consequence identify with the group and place a degree of emotional investment in its future development. This should not imply harmony – in fact establishing rules and norms by definition implies the existence of transgression. So at this stage there will be people who react against certain accepted norms in one way or another. They may be pushed into the role of 'scapegoat' by the group, which disapproves of their lack of conformity. They may be pressured into compliance, or they may emerge as new leaders, so altering basic group norms.

The group leaders should now be less overtly involved in controlling the direction of the group, and perhaps be providing more in terms of comment and feedback on what they see happening. This is partly in order to allow them to 'check' with the rest of the members as to whether their own perceptions are correct. The leaders will make comments such as 'I feel the group is angry about something, I'm not sure what it is, but perhaps other people sense it also?' or 'I feel the group is concentrating upon things that people are saying rather than the way in which people are feeling, which appears to be quite different because . . .' Other members will either agree or challenge the comments, and express the feelings they were unable to talk about. They might not be able to do this if the leader had made statements about the group mood such as 'The group is very angry because Colin arrived late'.

Performing. This is the stage at which the group has managed to develop through its normative processes and changes in role structure, and concentrates upon the major task it has to perform in relation to its individual members, and its own development. Much of this also occurs during the 'norming' stage, and the distinction is often temporal rather than structure.

Mourning. All groups have to end, and some have a natural life, e.g. during the school holidays or during a stay in hospital, and some have deliberately imposed time limits. All endings engender feelings in individuals, and it is important that the group leaders should be aware of this and give opportunities for people to deal with them effectively. There will be a sense of loss and rejection on the part of members when they realise the life of the group is near its end. This may precipitate reactions of withdrawal, or attempts to arrange to see members individually, or informally outside the formal group. The leader should encourage the members to discuss their feelings about ending the group, and allow them to summarise the group development as they see it. They may wish to continue formally, and the leaders may well find it possible and useful to do so, but this will require a return to the planning stage, to decide exactly what the aims and objectives for extending the group might be. Leaders might feel guilty at ending a group, particularly if it was successful, but clearly this is not a reason to prolong its life.

Recording and evaluating groupwork

As with other areas of social work, recording provokes a variety of responses in workers and clients, many of which are unfavourable. Most clients understandably object to details of intimate discussion being written and filed away. Even so, recording is particularly useful for groupworkers assessing a group's development, and in addition, provides the agency with evidence that a valid form of social work is actually taking place! The groupworkers may be helped to assess their own involvement in the group process when they write up, and account for happenings during group sessions, and they should certainly be able to assess individual members' progress. The recording may possibly be made available to the whole group for discussion and referred to as a group 'diary'.

5

Forming Impressions of People: The Problem of Accuracy

Introduction

This chapter is concerned with some of the factors involved in forming impressions of other people – judging for example how trustworthy or emotionally stable they are, or how well they can cope on their own – and, in particular, with making such judgements more accurately. Social workers are professional judges of people in this sense, and any increase in accuracy of understanding others and in predicting their behaviour is likely to be both more effective and more just.

Predictions of what other people are like and how they will behave are often accurate (e.g. Kenrick and Funder, 1988, Funder, 1987), but there is also room for improvement. Two points about the notion of 'good judges of personality' are provocative here. First, the idea of a 'good judge' implies accuracy with all kinds of personal qualities in all kinds of people with all kinds of evidence. Such all-purpose judges have not been found so far and the required versatility does, on reflection, seem unlikely. Rather, people probably tend to specialise, e.g. being good at judging depression in middle-aged men, but being less good at other judgements (Forgas, 1985).

Second, the evidence on what 'good judges' are like (which is, not surprisingly, confused) suggests that accuracy, in some people at least, is associated with

92

qualities which are not valued in western culture, e.g. passivity and social anxiety. One possible explanation is that accurate knowledge of others is disagreeable and causes those who see them accurately to withdraw. This is of course a pessimistic view of what people in general are like. Another explanation is that those in less powerful positions have a greater need to be accurate perceivers, because of their greater vulnerability. This is an explanation in terms of motives more than simply skill or intrinsic differences in ability. However, it is also possible that some good judges (in a fairly general sense) are calm, open-minded, etc. (Smith, 1973).

Questions about 'good judges' await further research, but meanwhile judgements continue to be made. The approach taken here is to review some of the sources of bias in our judgements and suggest approaches to counteracting them, and therefore improving accuracy. First, the general nature of perception is touched on. Second, the following factors within the general process of perception are discussed: the speed, richness and disproportionate power of first impressions; similarity; stereotypes, using physical attractiveness and gender as examples; place; implicit theories of personality; 'Barnum' statements; and non-verbal communication. Third, some general suggestions on how to increase accuracy (drawing in part on specific ideas from the first two sections of this chapter) are made. And fourth, the current position in personality theory is outlined, with particular emphasis on psychological type theory.

The general nature of perception

Seeing, hearing and our other senses are so familiar that it takes a leap of the imagination to realise their complexity (Gregory, 1977). The process of seeing, for example, includes upside-down images on our eyes and this information passing to the brain in the form of electrical impulses. When people have worn special glasses which invert the images – in a sense put them the right way up – they have adapted to the glasses in about a week, seeing things as they normally do. This phenomenon also illustrates what has been called the 'effort after meaning', which we habitually make to the extent of seeing meaning where there is very unlikely to be any. This is a central, creative aspect of forming impressions (and of being human), but also makes misjudgements possible.

Perception seems like taking a series of photographs but is really much more like making a sketch or a cartoon. Selection is inevitable. The benefits of being selective include reducing the strain on attention and memory, an economy which enables us for example to listen to one conversation (or bits of two) in a room full of conversations. A tape-recorder cannot do this. On the other hand, being selective may also mean missing crucial bits of information, and it makes prejudice possible.

Other sources of inaccurate impressions

First impressions

Impressions tend to be formed very quickly and almost automatically. Just a name sometimes suggests a certain kind of person: expecting something from all people called Judith, for example, because of one Judith in your life. Allport (1961) suggests that if you merely glance at a stranger and then let yourself imagine (perhaps with eyes closed) what they are like, a wealth of associations will probably appear.

We also tend to pay most attention to our first impressions, treating them as revealing the 'real person' and tending to see later, discrepant information as unrepresentative: 'Jenny is very friendly normally, she was tired today', because she was friendly the first time we met her, or in the first few minutes of the first meeting. This effect (the primary effect) is easy to counteract, with a simple warning enough for most people. However, there may then be a recency effect of underestimating the early evidence.

The most direct way of countering the disproportionate power of first impressions is first to become aware of them and then to treat them as hypotheses – to check the evidence on which they are based, and to look for further evidence. Less obviously, look for evidence supporting the *opposite* hypothesis (Lord *et al.*, 1984). A further strategy is to look for alternative interpretations of any evidence gathered, e.g. someone who avoids eye-contact may be shy, afraid (realistically or not), deep in thought, dishonest, or have learned not to look people, or certain kinds of people, in the eye.

In general terms, the strategies described above all suggest suspending belief in one's first judgements until sufficient information has been gathered. How much is 'sufficient'? It depends, but a crude extrapolation from Epstein's (1979) research suggests finding three supporting pieces of evidence before accepting a particular judgement. The supervisor at a holiday camp who judged me a 'good worker' on the basis of a surprise visit in which she found me polishing vigorously, would have been more accurate if she had tried three or more surprise visits and had considered alternative explanations, e.g. novelty of the task, energetic mood.

Strong liking or disliking at first meeting is particularly likely to be an inaccurate and unjust reaction, based on reacting to the person as if they are somebody else. The following six steps are developed from co-counselling (e.g. Evison and Horobin, 1988). In co-counselling or at least one approach to it, the steps are carried out openly in the relationship. In other situations they will generally be carried out privately, at a later time, or to yourself, in the interview, using all the spare capacity mentioned on p. 37!

(1) Ask 'Who does this person remind me of?'
(2) In what way is she/he (the new person) like X? Find as many specific similarities as possible, e.g. not 'his appearance', but 'the way he holds his head'.
(3) What do I want to say to X?
(4) Say it.
(5) In what ways is the new person not like X? Again, look for specific differences.
(6) Say 'This is Y, not X'.

The idea, of course, is to see the new person more clearly. It is also possible to suggest that this kind of confusion may be happening to a client who is reacting very strongly to you, and then, if appropriate, to take them through the six steps. See discussion of immediacy on p. 46.

Similarity

Both small and large similarities are attractive in another person, e.g. their liking for coffee, speed of thought, sense of humour. This may be because it feels good to have our views confirmed, because we anticipate that if someone agrees with us they are more likely to like us, because we feel more likely to be understood, etc. For accuracy of judgement, it means simply to beware of the 'like me' bias – of immediate positive judgements based on similarity. Further, it is an argument for trying to expand one's range of experiences, for the value of self-help groups, and for ex-sufferers from a particular problem working with current sufferers. The latter idea can however quickly become impractical.

We also tend to reject and dislike people who we see as being different from ourselves. This *might* be part of 'human nature'. If so, it would be most efficient to encourage people to group accordingly, something which already happens informally, and which for couple relationships is the basis of computer-dating. Alternatively, the tendency could be resisted, perhaps through encounter groups and multicultural education. If it is fear of being disagreed with that is crucial, then expressing beliefs and attitudes tentatively might help, because it is less rejecting. Consider also sometimes raising the issue of dissimilarity with a client: 'I wonder if the fact that you're young and I'm older is affecting us.' See section on 'immediacy' on p. 46. For discussions of prejudice and practical ways of reducing it, e.g. equal status and being involved in common tasks, see Aronson (1988, Chapter 5) and Dominelli (1988).

Stereotypes

Stereotypes are the extreme misuse of categories: a person is judged on the basis of one quality, e.g. age, sex, race, occupation, when people of for instance the same age are not similar in personality any more than most psychologists are romantic and dashing or most Russians cold. Two of the most obvious 'pieces of information' about most people new to us are their physical attractiveness and their gender. Both are correspondingly often used to stereotype.

Physical attractiveness. One stereotype that appears to be held very generally is that 'what is beautiful is good' (e.g. Aronson, 1988). It appears at an early age: even nursery school children tend to prefer their more attractive peers. Similarly, people have been asked to judge reports of 'rather severe' classroom disturbances, apparently described by a teacher. Photographs of the child who caused the trouble were attached to the reports. The judges all saw the same reports but the photograph, of a physically attractive or unattractive child, varied. The effect was a tendency to place more blame on unattractive children – 'a real problem' – than attractive – 'a bad day . . . her cruelty . . . need not be taken too seriously'. Such results may seem disconcerting; they are obviously unjust. A slightly more positive note is that although there is general agreement on which people are most attractive, there is some variation too.

'Beautyism' has been found in many studies and in a wide variety of settings. Allowing for it in judgements of others should be a step towards greater accuracy. I also suggest exploring your reactions to physically attractive and unattractive clients, and evaluating your own attractiveness in this respect, e.g. what effect does your evaluation have on your relationships? Is there any action that you can take, treating your own attractiveness as a 'problem to be managed' in the way discussed in Chapter 3?

Gender. Another potent source of error is stereotyping on the basis of gender, presumably because this too is a particularly obvious fact about most people. However, psychological sex differences are non-existent or very slight: there is considerable overlap even on highly stereotyped qualities like gentleness and physical aggression (Nicholson, 1984; Tavris and Wade, 1984) to the extent that to study 'sex differences' makes little sense, except as a contribution towards reducing the stereotypes. Consider for example Castleman's (1988) comment – and the evidence – on men, women and sexuality: 'Their patterns of sexual arousal are similar, their sex problems share identical causes and solutions, and their orgasms are, when described subjectively, indistinguishable' (p. 125).

The largest psychological sex difference known to me is part of the theory outlined in a later section (p. 104). About 70 per cent of women prefer Feeling (and 30 per cent of men), with about 60 per cent of men preferring Thinking (30 per cent of women) (Myers and McCaulley, 1985). The terms are technical ones, defined in that section. The important point here is that there are large proportions of people who do not fit with the culturally accepted stereotypes, even with so large a difference.

Place

Judgements made in pleasant rooms tend to be more positive than those made in ugly ones. For example, it has been suggested that strip-lighting makes judgements like 'hostile' – by clients and social workers – more likely. Perhaps interviews should be conducted by candlelight! A related factor is that impressions can also be affected by the mood of the person judging as well as the mood of the person judged.

'Implicit personality theories'

These are people's own theories about 'human nature' and 'personality', called implicit because often we are not aware of them, or take them for granted. They suggest that certain qualities are related, for example that inconsiderate people are also irritable and cold, that warm people are also generous and witty. These may or may not be true, either in general or for a particular person. Different people's implicit theories are contradictory, so that at least some of them must be inaccurate (Cook, 1979; Forgas, 1985).

For improving accuracy, the principle is to look out for inferences from one characteristic to another, or – more simply – to ask what the basis is for each judgement of a characteristic, thus by-passing any implicit theory. A related strategy – because theories are also decisions about which aspects of reality to concentrate on and which to ignore – is to look for your favourite qualities. These may not be very useful for understanding some other people, indeed they may not apply at all. Look for example at the qualities that come most readily to mind when writing a report or a reference. Why these qualities?

'Barnum' statements

Barnum statements are terms used to describe personality which appear to be individual but are not. They are used by many different kinds of people, including astrologers and clinical psychologists (Bayne, 1980). They occur in 'case' discussions. Some examples: 'She has a great deal of unused capacity which she has not turned to her advantage', 'Security is one of his major goals in life', 'He feels great sometimes, other times like hiding away'.

The problem with such statements is that they can impede real understanding, giving a misplaced sense of confidence and reducing appropriate doubt. The remedy is to make them more concrete and individual, e.g. how exactly does this person express insecurity? Also, beware of their seductiveness! For example, if a palmist says something about your personality, try asking yourself if it is true of two friends as well as yourself. If it is, it is best to ignore it as a statement about you as an individual.

Non-verbal communication (NVC)

Valuable information can be observed and conveyed non-verbally, especially as NVC tends to operate outside or on the fringe of consciousness and is therefore more difficult to fake than words. It is the likely basis of many first impressions: 'There was something about her', 'It was just a feeling'. It gives human communication both great versatility and great capacity for confusion. And it emphasises the fact that each of us *is* our body; it is not like a horse, with us the rider (Rowan, 1983, p. 71).

'Channels' of NVC can be categorised as follows:

(1) The way we use space, including touch (technically known as proxemics).
(2) Movements, gestures and expressions (kinesics).
(3) More static aspects of the body and surroundings.
(4) Aspects of speech other than words: tone, loudness, pauses, etc. (paralanguage).

Use of space. How close people like to be physically to others varies; it matters who the other person is and what the situation is, but there are also consistent general preferences, and class, sex and race differences in these, e.g. people from South America, Arab countries and Pakistan stand closest, those from the UK, USA and Sweden farthest (Argyle, 1988). This is not a trivial matter: it can lead to misunderstandings, with a kind of dance taking place, the pursuing person interpreting the other's behaviour as cold and unfriendly, the pursued finding the other too 'pushy'.

Preferences in seating arrangements also exist. It has been suggested, for example, that chairs placed across the corner of a desk are preferred by clients in general to chairs across a desk or without a desk. Touch is a closely related NVC; again some marked cultural differences have been found. With a particular person, a pat on the arm may be a powerful way of making contact – especially if you do it 'naturally' – or it may be strongly resented as patronising or intrusive (Brenner, 1982). It may also be very unhelpful, e.g. touching someone to stop them crying because *you* feel uncomfortable. Consider exploring your own views on touch (cf. Older, 1977).

Gestures, etc. Some gestures give fairly straightforward information – 'Come here', for example, and 'No'. They are a kind of sign-language. Of much more interest are unintentional gestures, especially those that Ekman and Friesen (1975) refer to as 'leakage'. The idea is that sometimes true feelings leak out despite attempts to conceal them, e.g. saying you're not anxious but fidgeting a lot could indicate that you really are anxious.

There are many intriguing ideas about NVC, e.g. are flared nostrils and tight lips signs of tension and fear? What if there are accompanying signals of great confidence? Two states which have been investigated experimentally are depression and anxiety. Waxer (1978) videotaped admission interviews with psychiatric patients diagnosed as either depressed, not depressed, anxious or not anxious. Raters were able to identify these states from non-verbal cues alone: depressed patients made little eye-contact, had turned-down mouths, bowed heads, etc.; anxious patients moved their hands a lot or braced them unnaturally, bit or licked their lips, had stiff upper torsos, and so on; patients low on anxiety used their hands to gesture rather than fidget. This kind of research suggests the possibility of a very quick and unintrusive confirmation or check of judgements of emotional state, which may have implications for the next step in an interview. The evidence for other interpretations is poor (Argyle, 1988).

One of the most studied NVCs is 'eye-contact'. It is used in part to help regulate conversations. Normally one person talks and sometimes looks directly at the person who is listening, while the person listening looks at the person talking most of the time, until it is their turn to speak. Occasionally, two people's ways of indicating 'I want to speak' or 'It's your turn' take time to mesh. Eye-contact may also indicate interest or hostility, depending on other things, such as the topic of conversation.

Crying is another example of the ambiguity of NVCs. Mills and Wooster (1987) suggest marked individual differences in the form it takes at its peak: from watery eyes to intense weeping to deep sobbing. They emphasise helping a client on the verge of tears (a) to cry, and (b) to identify the underlying emotions and tensions.

Static aspects of NVC. These include clothing, physique, even offices and buildings: what do your surroundings 'say'? Rowan (1988) and Storr (1979) discuss the effects of furnishings on interviews, suggesting some personal things for 'warmth' but nothing too revealing (like family photos or crucifixes) because they may inhibit communication.

On clothes, physique and characteristics like bowed lips and wearing glasses, there is consensus but not, as far as is known, accuracy. It may be true that 'By the age of 40 we have the face we deserve' (George Orwell) but it has not been demonstrated (Argyle, 1988). The important point about these stereotypes as far as increasing accuracy is concerned is to notice any tendencies towards them in yourself, and to question them.

Paralanguage. Novelists have to convey paralanguage and other channels of NVC verbally, e.g. '"You're really amazing", she said irritably.' Again there is consensus on what different inflections, volume, etc. mean, but probably not accuracy. On current evidence what matters most is knowing how other people tend to react to your tone, face and other NVC, and how you tend to react to theirs, and to make allowances or adjustments accordingly (see Ekman and Friesen 1975, Chapter 12).

Berne (1966) makes the point dramatically, suggesting a 'rule of facial mimicry which has played an important part in determining the destinies of individuals and even nations'. The rule is: 'The visual impact (on the onlooker) of small movements or changes of the facial musculature is greater than their kinaesthetic impact (on the subject).' Thus very small movements of certain muscles, which seems insignificant or are not even noticed by the person making them, may be obvious to the person looking. Imagine feeling sleepy and trying to conceal this from a client. Berne suggests the following test: droop your eyelids to what seems to you a negligible extent and then examine the effect in a mirror. He further points out that the effect shows even when you are on your own, i.e. when your attention is not also occupied in speaking to someone.

The main problem in interpreting NVC accurately is its ambiguity. However, *changes* from a person's characteristic

NVC are more likely to be significant, e.g. their face 'lighting up' when talking about a particular person or topic. For general purposes, Scheflen's (1964) analogy is appropriate: 'a letter of the alphabet does not carry meaning until it is part of a word which is part of a sentence which is part of a discourse and a situation' (p. 324). NVCs are the letters, and sometimes a bit more; interpretations, when they are made, should be very tentative.

Interpretations can also be at different levels. Consider a client who is swinging her foot (F). You can note F and just bear it in mind. You can say to the client: 'You're angry' (strong interpretation) or 'I think F suggests perhaps that you're angry?' (probably more appropriately gentle). Alternatively, and without interpreting, 'Can you say what F means to you?', or 'Try stopping F, and putting your foot on the ground. What happens?'

Increasing accuracy of judgement: general principles

Two general principles are suggested. Both try to counter the taken-for-granted, 'natural' element in perception. It may also help to know that there are other factors than those touched on above which work against accuracy: politeness and ingratiation for example, and what the other person thinks of you, and what they think you think of them.

(1) Try to separate judgements and the evidence they're based on. This is discussed on p. 94 with reference to speed of first impressions. Essentially, it is treating early judgements as hypotheses, and slowing down the normal process. Remember how easy it is to over-generalise from one piece of evidence: 'That was a really good book' (when it was one idea or sentence you liked, or had read!) or 'She's tremendous' (one kind action, one stimulating remark). So look for themes, e.g. if someone is calm on three occasions, then the term 'calm' is quite well supported, especially if a variety of situations is involved.

(2) When talking with clients, look for alternative interpretations of the evidence and test their adequacy. In
particular, consider how influential the situation
(including yourself) is, and the nature of your relationship with the client.

A further strategy is to question and add to one's
categories and implicit theories: the better your theory, the
more quickly and accurately you will understand someone.
Unfortunately, there is as yet no generally accepted theory
of personality in psychology – no firm answer to the issue of
the best way to describe a person. The next section outlines
one approach, 'psychological type' theory, first putting it in
a general context.

'Psychological type'

The position in personality theory described by Allport
many years ago, that 'everyone, it seems, knows what
personality is, but no-one can precisely describe it' (1937),
is still true. There is an immense variety of personality
theories, none of them generally accepted in psychology. In
broad terms, the theories correspond to the major
approaches to counselling, i.e. psychodynamic, cognitive-
behavioural and humanistic. The exception is trait theories.
There is a trait perspective on counselling (Costa and
McCrae, 1986) but it is not generally seen as a major force,
at least not in textbooks.

Trait theory is itself diverse. Indeed there are many
hundreds of traits and possible traits, only a few of them
studied at all intensively, and there are competing ways of
organising the traits into a smaller and more manageable
number of higher order traits. In addition there are some
traits, e.g. extraversion, which are well-known but not well
understood, partly because of conflicting definitions.

I have chosen to emphasise Myers' (1980) psychological
type theory for a number of reasons. First, it shows a very
encouraging relationship with one of the most prominent trait
theories (five factor theory, e.g. Costa and McCrae, 1986).

This is encouraging because the two approaches have reached close agreement using different methodologies and coming from different traditions (Dachowski, 1987). Second, type theories are used by most people – and for good reason: they are *sufficiently* general to be useful, more like temperaments or styles, and not like Barnum statements. Third, *this* type theory is (a) positive – it focuses on strength and potential strengths, (b) useful at various levels of complexity, (c) a theory of personality development and change as well as of description, (d) widely applicable, (e) so far quite well supported, and (f) accompanied by a measure – the Myers–Briggs Type Indicator – which is consistent with it and psychometrically sound.

Myers (1980) developed and clarified some of Jung's (1923) ideas about basic personality differences. Like Jung, she did not use the term type in a static, 'pigeon-holing' sense: rather, the categories are 'compass points . . . in the wilderness of the psyche' (Jung). It follows – and was emphasised by Myers and others – that there is a lot more to a person than their type, but that type is a good starting point for understanding others and oneself. In particular, discovering one's psychological type can be a very positive experience. Two of the preferences helped me make sense of aspects of myself which had puzzled and sometimes disturbed me for years, and to value them.

Myers was also concerned with the 'constructive use of differences'. She wanted people to value the opposite strengths to their own. As an example, one of my students, an extravert, used to dismiss introverts as dull and uninteresting; now, after working on type theory, she sees them as inclined to reflection and as liking more time alone. She has also changed her behaviour – writing a note to an introverted colleague rather than bouncing in without warning to see her.

The preferences

The central concept in type theory is 'preference'. Preferences are elements of inner self-awareness which may or may not be expressed in behaviour, and consequences of expressing or not expressing them are suggested. For example, taking one of the preferences, the theory suggests that people with a preference for extraversion tend to behave in an extraverted way: to be more active, outgoing, sociable and expressive. However, a few people will have a preference for extraversion but not have developed – used and trusted – it sufficiently to actually behave in an extraverted manner much of the time. In effect they will be 'unfulfilled extraverts': predominantly quiet, private, reserved and inward, behaving, at least to the casual observer, like genuine introverts. They – and 'unfulfilled introverts' – will, according to the theory, have less 'sense of self' and be less effective.

Preferences are what a person feels is most comfortable and 'natural' for them. It is only when preferences are actually used and trusted – developed – that the behaviours and attitudes listed in the next section tend to be associated with them. Most people have developed their preferences, or most of their preferences, to a significant degree (Myers and McCaulley, 1985). In this section I will give an indication of the types as a way of describing personality. Type theory as a model of personality development is discussed in Myers (1980) and Bayne (1988).

Type theory suggests four pairs of preferences:

Extraversion (E)	– Introversion (I)
Sensing (S)	– Intuition (N)
Thinking (T)	– Feeling (F)
Judging (J)	– Perceiving (P)

The theory further suggests that everyone uses all eight preferences each day but that we prefer and tend to be more skilful with one of each pair, and therefore can usefully be characterised as, for example, an ESFJ or an ISTJ. There are sixteen combinations of four preferences, and therefore sixteen psychological types. You may like to guess your own type on the basis of the descriptions below.

As indicated above, Extraversion includes the idea of energy directed towards the external world, including preferences for being with other people and for action. People with a developed preference for extraversion tend to be more active, outgoing, sociable and expressive. Conversely, Introversion includes a preference for reflection and a need to be alone to recover from social contact. Introverts tend to be more inward, private and reserved. Social contact may be enjoyed but it is also draining. E and I are very rich concepts in this theory (see e.g. Bayne, 1988).

If you prefer Sensing (S) to Intuition (N), it is more likely that (among other qualities) you are realistic and practical, want to see and touch things, trust and remember facts, work steadily, and are more observant than imaginative. This fairly standard description of the S preference was recently criticised, by an ISFP, as 'pale and plodding', and the sort of description one would expect from people who prefer the opposite function (N). In his view, well-developed S is much more: it includes for example using all the senses in a clear, pure way, and really looking and listening. Intuition (called N for short to avoid confusion with introversion) is to a large extent the opposite of S. It is centrally concerned with possibilities and speculation, with patterns and links between ideas, and with inspiration.

Thinking (T) and Feeling (F) are two ways of judging or making decisions. One emphasises facts, the other feelings. If you prefer T, it is more likely that (among other qualities) you try to be fair, logical and clear, are brief and businesslike, give and seek criticism, find ideas and things more interesting than people, and treat emotional relationships and ideals as less central to life than do people with a developed preference for F. T does *not* correlate with academic intelligence, and does *not* mean an absence of emotion – it is more a matter of emphasis, and a greater likelihood of asking 'Is it true?' rather than 'Do I like it?' – which is more an F question. Fs tend to be more interested in feelings, to need harmony, to be warm and trusting, to appreciate, and to make decisions on the basis of likes and dislikes (values).

The final pair of preferences, Judging (J) and Perceiving (P), are associated with being more organised and decisive, and preferring to plan (J), and being flexible and easy-going (P).

Talking about type/thinking in type terms

The terms used above were carefully chosen to be as unbiased towards the opposite preferences as possible. However, skilful use of type terms involves using terms which make sense to a particular client, and treating the terms as hypotheses which may or may not be useful. Most terms describing preferences or types can be expressed in the form 'People tend to be more X or more Y. Do you think either is more true of you?' For example, 'People tend to be either reflective or active. Does either word fit you better?' This approach emphasises the principles of (a) preference rather than pigeon-holing, and (b) all preferences and types being valuable.

Ethical use of the measure associated with type theory, the Myers–Briggs Type Indicator (MBTI), requires specialised training, partly because the MBTI is a psychological measure and partly because type theory is unusual and quite complicated. However, parts of the theory can be of immediate practical use without a deep understanding of it, and without the MBTI.

Type and communication

According to type theory, all types can communicate well with each other but difference in type is sometimes a cause of misunderstandings, rejection and hostility. Opposite types can be the enemy! A useful starting point is 'X and Y are different, and that might suggest a way of communicating better', rather than 'I just can't stand ESTJs!' The general sources of conflict between I and E are sociability and privacy. Between S and N, they are Ss being seen as or feeling slow and mundane, Ns as impractical and unobservant.

Similarly, Fs can see Ts as unsympathetic and critical, Ts can see Fs as illogical and too soft. For example, someone who preferred F might make a request on the basis of 'I'd like to . . .' when their T manager would, typically, want reasons. Js and Ps tend to clash on issues of order and autonomy (Myers and McCaulley, 1985). Meetings are excellent arenas for observing these differences.

Temperament theory

Psychological type theory is complicated, with central roles for personality development, a distinction between preferences and behaviour, and interactions between the preferences. However, several simpler levels of description are useful (Myers and McCaulley, 1985). Keirsey and Bates (1978), for example, suggest four temperaments, each identified by two pairs of preferences: SP, SJ, NT and NF. For example 'SP' covers the following four psychological types: ISFP, ISTP, ESFP and ESTP. The following paragraphs summarise the expected relationships between temperament and aspects of work. They are developed from Keirsey and Bates (1973), Stewart (1987), and other sources. They appear to be useful on the basis of personal experience and observation, but have not been adequately tested as yet.

Temperament and most-liked aspects of work (and/or leisure)

SP: Emergencies and pressure. Solving practical problems, perhaps in a high risk, tense environment. Variety, a lot going on. 'Adaptable realists'.

SJ: Meeting deadlines, resolving issues and problems, in a structured and stable environment. Attending to details. Planning well in advance. To be socially concerned and accepted. Security. 'Realistic decision-makers.'

NT: Producing new, high quality ideas. Being respected for their ideas and achievements by people they respect. Autonomy. 'Logical and ingenious.'

NF: Helping others in a 'nurturing' way. Being a resource. Being approved of and supported in a stimulating and harmonious environment. Making full use of their own talents. Being 'energised through accomplishments'. 'Enthusiastic and insightful.'

Temperament and least-liked/most stressful aspects of work (and/or leisure)

SP: Not much happening. Monotony. Unclear or no information. Lack of freedom (Unclear objectives matter much less.)

SJ: Unclear objectives. Changes of plan. Ambiguity. Lack of control.

NT: Doing routine and repetitive things, especially if they are detailed as well. Bureaucracy. Difficult relationships.

NF: Conflict. Saying no. Depressed and suicidal people. Criticism.

Temperament and expected reactions to stress

SP: Frivolity, flight, 'go own way', breakdown.

SJ: Redefine objectives, more resources, double check, more control, dogmatic.

NT: Over-work, fight, intolerance, conform rebelliously, pedantic debate.

NF: Self-sacrifice, cynicism, hysteria, depression.

If any of the categories 'fit' you, they provide a check on any queries you made earlier about your own type. The best starting point however is to complete the MBTI or to train in its use (address at end of chapter).

Criticisms of the MBTI and type theory

There are some more equivocal aspects of the MBTI and of type theory. Some of these apply to all personality measures, e.g. that the MBTI is crude, can be faked, measures only some aspects of personality, and that there are other practical and important measures and theories. Two criticisms are slightly more serious: that the MBTI measures preferences, not how developed the preferences are, and that some people get ambiguous scores on the

MBTI, i.e. their type according to the measure and to themselves is not clear.

The first criticism is a problem in research with the MBTI rather than for the applications and aspects discussed above, especially as a measure of preference is less threatening than a measure of development. On the second criticism, ambiguous scores can be resolved in a variety of ways – through exercises, asking people who 'know you well', and careful observation. For example, taking T and F, do you tend to like/dislike and then perhaps analyse and criticise (developed Feeling preference) or to analyse and criticise and then perhaps evaluate (developed Thinking preference)? And which, generally, do you feel most comfortable with: valuing (for or against) or analysis/criticism?

It is also possible to see yourself as more than one 'type'. However, although in terms of the type model of development older people are more likely to have developed all their preferences anyway, this is only up to a point: in theory each person has a 'true type', which is them at their most natural and effective, and which remains the same throughout their life.

Conclusions

The general conclusion for this chapter echoes that for Chapter 3: improving accuracy of judgement is a demanding task but there are a variety of strategies to choose from and the effort seems worthwhile. Psychological type is a very rich approach with some unusual merits. At the very least it suggests in a concrete way how difficult empathy can be (because the preferences are pairs of opposites). But I see it as much more than that: as a particularly valuable approach to developing realistic self-esteem and to understanding and valuing others more.

For more information on the MBTI and training, contact Oxford Psychologists Press, Lambourne House, 311–321 Banbury Road, Oxford, OX2 7JH.

6

Developmental Psychology and Socialisation: Understanding the Human Life Course

In this chapter we want to review the contribution of developmental psychology and socialisation theories to understanding human development through the life course. This is the area in which a psychodynamic approach is usually favoured by social work trainers. We consider that academic psychology has much to offer also, and this should be made explicit to social work students and practitioners.

Developmental psychology and socialisation

Although most of what is termed 'developmental psychology' is about infancy and childhood, there has been a recent interest in adulthood as a stage of development. This has emerged from psychological studies of infertility (Woollett, 1987), motherhood (Nicolson, 1988), fatherhood (Lewis, 1986) and studies of the family (Vetere and Gale, 1987). Even so there is still an increasing emphasis on the study of the first two years of life (Bremner, 1988). Despite an emphasis on cognitive or behavioural aspects of development, recent writers have argued for the value of taking social context into account (Richards and Light, 1986). Thus there are increasing attempts to take emotional aspects of human development as seriously as the cognitive and behavioural ones.

Although a crucial area of knowledge, socialisation sits uncomfortably between sociology and psychology. Its focus is upon how individuals become social and gain under-standing of society and their own place within that society, and as such it has to carry difficulties inherent in both disciplines, Sociology's focus on the social at the expense of the individual, and Psychology's focus on the individual over the social. Some efforts have been made to overcome these problems.

The work of Leonard (1984) is noteworthy here in attempting to explain the importance of social class, race and gender in socialisation. Socialisation is also about the acquisition of social skills and managing relationships with others. Research is clearly a complex matter, and it is the longitudinal studies such as those by the Newsons (e.g. 1976) and Rutter *et al.* (1989) which account for the development of psychological characteristics in a social context that are particularly useful.

This chapter reviews the areas of immediate concern in social work practice. We shall begin with moral develop-ment as making moral judgements is an integral part of the social work task; then go on to look at theories of loss and change, and thirdly gender issues in development.

Moral behaviour and development

A central problem in social work is that of morality. This is important for assessing the relationship between the individ-ual client's behaviour and the rules and values of a particular society; but perhaps more fundamental is the set of moral principles which surrounds the practitioner's role as an agent of control. Psychologists have examined the ways in which individuals come to identify and learn social rules, and how they organise their consequent behaviour.

Anthropological studies have revealed a consistency of particular rules which govern behaviour, and are of the kind that affect survival and the continuation of that society. These are referred to as moral rules and set the basis for values and social culture. The issues which are of universal concern are things such as danger to oneself and others, property and ownership, hygiene, control, sexuality, aggression, support for individuals and the group, honesty, and respect for authority.

It may be argued that social workers are 'guardians' of society's moral rules, particularly in relation to mental health work, child care, working with offenders, and in various kinds of community work, where the social worker may well be holding the balance between certain influential individuals and groups within the community. Thus social workers are in the position of being representatives of society, which includes the individual apparently transgressing the rules, and having the power to make or influence judgements about the action which should be taken.

This book is concerned with the psychological rather than philosophical aspects of morality, and therefore makes a contribution to the way social workers might understand behaviour and the reasoning behind it. Behavioural, social-learning, psychoanalytic and cognitive-developmental approaches to psychology, all confront these issues (see the description of these approaches in Chapter 1).

The behavioural approach

Behavioural psychologists are concerned with the way people act, rather than the way they reason about morality. They propose that a person's obedience to a culture's moral rules depends on the *consequences* of doing so, or not doing so, that is, the punishments or rewards that ensue. They consider that behaviour that provides rewards in a given situation is likely to be repeated in a similar situation, and behaviour that is punished is less likely to be repeated. Thus individuals who are punished for breaking the law are less likely to do so again. However psychologists (e.g. Thorndyke, Watson, Skinner and others) have found that if acceptable ways of behaviour are to be learnt, it is important for the rewards or punishments to be administered immediately after the behaviour.

Most psychologists would probably consider that reward is preferable to punishment in child rearing, because punishment merely suppresses behaviour. It does not provide long-term inner control. Studies have also demonstrated that it is likely to create hostility, which may well increase antisocial activities in those who receive too much punishment.

The social learning approach

This develops an exploration of behaviour in relation to moral rules. In one famous experiment by Bandura, the importance of modelling behaviour for young children was developed. They used nursery-school children for subjects, and divided them into experimental and control groups. The children in the experimental group watched an adult spend several minutes mistreating a doll – punching it, standing on it, pulling its hair, and eventually banging it with a mallet. Then the groups were allowed to play with some attractive toys, which were soon taken away from them, and they were told that other children were going to play with them. This was clearly a very frustrating situation, which Bandura intended should initiate aggression.

At this stage, all the children were given a doll and a mallet to play with, as well as 'aggressive' toys such as darts and guns. Both the experimental group and the control group were observed through a one-way mirror for 20 minutes. The experimental group expressed their aggression on the whole by an imitation of the adult: by mistreating the doll. The control group were also aggressive, but did not adopt this behaviour: they made more use of the guns and the darts.

This explanation of behaviour may well be important in practice for breaking the pattern of aggressive parenting by individuals who themselves were physically abused by their own parents. According to the social-learning theorists, they would have learned a particular style of parenting which is aggressive, and to react to frustrations by hitting their children. By providing day care for children who have been attacked by their parents, it should be possible to provide a stronger alternative model for parenting behaviour. As discussed in Chapter 1, it might be the *qualities* possessed by the model rather than their importance in a child's life which makes them effective. A warm, caring nursery teacher or residential worker may be more influential than an aggressive parent.

Bandura also suggested that individuals do not learn about moral rules in response to their exposure to reward or punishment, but by observation of other people's behaviour. By watching other people individuals witness the consequences of their actions and the behaviour that they assess to be appropriate under certain conditions.

The cognitive-developmental approach

It is important to try to understand how individuals *reason* about moral rules. Jean Piaget (1932) and Lawrence Kohlberg (1969) concerned themselves with this. Piaget had based his research on children's thinking about *intent* in moral issues. He worked with children aged between 6 and 12 and told them pairs of stories about childish transgressions, asking them which action was the naughtier and why. The pairs of stories might be as follows:

(1) There was a little boy called John, who thought he would help his mummy by cleaning the kitchen. While he was doing this he knocked a pile of plates over, and they all broke.
(2) William's mummy told him never to play in the kitchen when she was not there, but one day he did, and knocked over a cup and cracked it.

Who was the naughtier and why!

Younger children usually insisted that John was the naughtier because the *consequences* of his action were more severe. Piaget found that they did understand that he was trying to help, but were still more concerned about the amount of damage. He calls this type of reasoning 'objective responsibility', meaning that actions are judged on the basis of their material outcome rather than their intent. He also demonstrated that children's first views grow out of their relationship to adults as authority figures. They are subordinate to adults, and believe that rules emanate from sources *outside* themselves, which adults recognise and thus forbid and punish. He refers to this stage as 'heteronomous morality'. When children grow older, free themselves from adult authority and mix more with their peer group, they begin to understand that rules are social agreements, accepted by all members of a group as a basis for co-operative action. This stage he refers to as one of 'autonomous morality'.

In the late 1960s Lawrence Kohlberg took Piaget's work on moral development as the basis for further research. He aimed to show that if cognitive development in human beings had a natural and normal development course, then moral reasoning may also demonstrate a normal pattern of development. This was based on the premiss that if the development of moral reasoning demonstrates a standard or universal form of development with increasing maturity, then the mature form of moral thinking can be considered to be better or more desirable than earlier forms of moral thought. Kohlberg attempted to describe the changes in children's moral thinking systematically, as they occur with development. He carried out a series of comparison studies of children of different ages, and a longitudinal study of a group of children as they grew up. The consistencies between these two studies gave him a firm basis for claiming that age group differences do reflect individual development in moral reasoning.

Kohlberg presented his subjects with a moral dilemma which presented a conflict between competing claims for justice. Their task was to choose a solution and explain their choice. After analysing the statements of children at various stages of development, he constructed a model of growth in moral reasoning. This consisted of 3 levels of morality, each of which could be divided into 2 stages, thus:

Level 1: preconventional morality. The level of most children under the age of 9, many adolescents, and some adult criminal offenders.

Stage 1: The individual at this stage conforms to avoid punishment from authority, whose power she/he accepts.

Stage 2: Self-interested exchanges. Individual conforms to get the most possible advantage for himself/herself.

Level 2: conventional morality. Most adolescents and adults are at this level. The individual now understands, accepts, and upholds social rules and expectations, especially those that emanate from authorities.

Stage 3: Maintaining good interpersonal relationships. The individual wants to be seen as good, and to live up to others' expectations. She/he will experience shame if seen in an unflattering light by important people.

Stage 4: Maintaining the social system. The individual agrees to a set of rules and obligations which are seen as justified in order for the system to operate.

Level 3: postconventional morality. Only a minority of adults reach this level, and then rarely until they are 20 or above. Individuals at this level internalise their own formulation of society's rules according to their own moral principles. When a person's principles are at odds with social rules, the person will be guided by their own.

Stage 5: Social contract and individual right. Social rules are seen as capable of being changed by those affected. A revolutionary leader might operate at this stage.

Stage 6: Universal ethical principles. Individuals recognise the universal ethical principles to which they have a sense of personal commitment. Compliance is based upon personal conscience, not external pressure or even social contract. A martyr, or a terrorist, willing to sacrifice their own life for their cause might be seen to operate at this stage.

Kohlberg says that these levels of morality reflect three different social orientations. Preconventional people have a concrete individual perspective on society; conventional people have a member of society's view; and postconventional people take a prior to society perspective. Only postconventional people ask themselves what kind of social regulations a society would have to develop if it were to start from scratch.

Kohlberg further predicted that moral reasoning was related to behaviour. He did a series of experiments to show that people at a high level of moral reasoning are less likely to administer shocks in experiments like Milgram's (see pp. 70–1). Another piece of work which used Kohlberg's stages showed that children at stage 3 are more likely to give way to group pressure than when they are at a higher stage. Also, that people at stages 5 and 6 were seen to be more likely to cheat than those at 3 and 4. Another study showed that university teachers of science and university administrators tended to employ law and order reasoning more than social science and humanities teachers.

The psychodynamic approach

This is based on the work of Freud, whose studies of developmental psychology led him to believe that structural reorganisation of the personality occurs at certain crucial points in development, and that these stages were universal features in the development of all human beings. Children want their wishes fulfilled immediately and flare up in anger if frustrated. They also show strong sexual passion. Freud felt that during socialisation antisocial impulses were brought under control, and moral development was a process of internalisation through which children move from external behavioural controls (rewards and punishments) to internal self-controls. This transition is closely linked with children's feelings towards their parents. Parental pressure towards socialisation makes children angry, and the thought of expressing this anger arouses their anxiety: partly because they might lose their parents. Children therefore repress their anger and turn it in on themselves. This is the foundation of 'guilt' – a powerful motivating force in development. The internalisation of the parents' (and thus society's) rules are embodied in the *superego* which is a harsh, punitive and inflexible psychological mechanism.

Theories of loss and change

Erikson's (1968) model of the life cycle relies upon the notion of change through a series of crises. Successfully overcoming these equips an individual with the skills and knowledge to cope with the subsequent demands of the next stage of life.

Central to his theory is that negotiation of a viable *identity* enables the individual to progress towards forming mature intimate relationships. Bowlby's (1988) work on 'attachment' and 'loss' has also contributed to knowledge of the psychological effects of insecurity derived from social impoverishment in infancy. Although there are real concerns about the validity and reliability of the empirical source of Bowlby's theory, concepts of 'attachment', 'loss' and 'change' are important for understanding life long human development and a crucial component of psychology for social workers.

Since Bowlby's early work in the 1940s, there has been a growing interest in infant attachment behaviour. Schaffer and Emerson's (1964) longitudinal study of 60 infants in Scotland showed that by the age of eighteen months they were each attached to about three people. In the very early days the infants demonstrate what they call 'indiscriminant attachment' although by the age of around six months they become wary of strangers. Rutter (1972) produced similar evidence and stressed that infants can form attachments to men. Tizard's (1975) study of children in their adoptive families demonstrated that it is frequently possible to overcome early emotional disturbance and separation with a stable, loving environment.

Separation and loss

Ainsworth (1960s and 1970s) used a series of observations of children of various ages to demonstrate the ways in which a mother's presence or absence can affect a child's behaviour and emotional security. She created a series of 'strange situations' where an infant and mother were in a room filled with toys. A stranger would enter, and the mother left shortly afterwards, having allowed time for the stranger to be introduced. It appeared that children stayed close to their mothers in the strange room, but soon moved to the toys, returning intermittently to establish contact. When the stranger entered, the child moved towards the mother, perhaps even hiding behind her, but most children warmed to the new person and responded to her efforts to play. When the mother left, however, most children showed distress and became less involved with play.

Ainsworth (1964) suggested that once children have been exposed to separation, they become sensitised in such a way that similar experiences are likely to be especially traumatic for them.

Douglas and Blomfield (1958), however, had found that long-term ill effects generally followed separation only when it was accompanied by a change of environment. Their study was related to hospitalisation of children, which indicates that the ill effects may be associated with the *context* of the environment rather than the change itself.

Marris (1986) developed Bowlby's ideas while also borrowing concepts from Piaget. He sees 'grief' as a response to loss of *meaning*, suggesting that it is provoked by all situations of loss, including social changes and any conditions which disrupt an individual's ability to make sense of their life.

Personal bereavement, then, is but one element of a process that occurs in more than one context. The psychological task is that of *reintegration*, which is essentially similar wherever and however the structures of meaning fall apart removing the predictability from an individual's world.

The work of Erikson, Bowlby and Murray-Parkes contributes to this framework which is useful for explaining various aspects of human development. Explanations of socialisation as a continuous process of loss and meaning and reintegration illuminates a life course model of psychological development informing social work practice.

In order to look at this more closely, we shall consider a traditional model of bereavement and the grief reaction.

Bereavement

Bereavement most frequently occurs from late middle age onwards. This kind of bereavement is usually concerned with the loss of a husband or wife, but clearly the distress and grief are also acute for a child who loses a parent or sibling, for parents who lose a child, or for anyone who loses a close friend. Although most social workers are involved with the elderly bereaved, and the major studies are concerned with this group, it is not a condition exclusive to the elderly. Similarly many of the reactions in bereavement are similar to those originally described by Bowlby who was concerned with loss and separation between parents and young children.

The grief reaction

Psychologists and psychiatrists have long been interested in bereavement and grief. As early as 1917 Freud stressed the psychological importance of mourning after bereavement. Grief and loss produce a mixture of physiological and psychological reactions which are closely bound up with the social pressures concerning a change in status. These are often accompanied by financial problems, particularly in the case of a widow whose husband was breadwinner, who may well not be adequately insured or able to earn a living.

Thus it is understandable that Colin Murray-Parkes (1972), who made a famous study of twenty-two London widows, and has taken a special interest in the concept of bereavement, suggests that grief is an illness. He justifies this by saying that the emotional and physiological symptoms cause people to go to their doctors for help because they experience physical discomfort and disturbance of function. Also, he says that newly bereaved people are often treated as sick by the rest of society. They are expected to miss work, to be visited by relatives, and have others take responsibility for major decisions. However, Murray-Parkes says that bereavement can also bring strength and maturity, and if a person copes with the 'challenge' of bereavement they may well change their view of the world and themselves. He described the stages of grief reaction, but shows that at each stage people are subject to a series of emotional conflicts and a variety of psychological reactions:

Searching. People experience 'pangs' of grief rather than prolonged pain, and will often cry out for their loved one. This reaction can begin within a few hours or days of the bereavement, and usually reaches a peak of severity within 5 to 14 days. Bowlby has called this the phase of yearning and protest. The bereaved person shows a lack of interest in normal life, and experiences a persistent, obtrusive search for the person who has gone. Most normal adults are fully aware that there is no point in searching for the dead person, but this does not prevent a strong impulse to search. Many experience illusions in which they see the dead person, or they will look for them in a crowd of people. Some people frequently return to the locations that were the favourite places of the dead to check whether or not they have really gone from them.

Mitigation. When people experience intense pining, something often happens to mitigate the grief and pain. Murray-Parkes says that this consists of some sort of sight or sound to give the impression that the 'search' is at an end. The commonest experience is that the dead person is nearby, and this provides a very comforting sensation for the bereaved. This experience was reported by fifteen of the twenty-two individuals in Murray-Parkes study. Also, many people experience hallucinations and dreams which include the dead person. They are often happy, but include the feeling that something is 'not quite well'. Other forms of mitigation include the bereaved person not believing the loss has occurred: waiting for the dead person to come home, or disagreeing with doctors and other relatives that the death has actually occurred.

Several people report a 'numbness' on receiving the news of death, and feelings of unreality, but these reactions tend to be transient. Many will try and avoid thoughts of the lost person, and avoid meeting people who might discuss them, or getting into situations which might be connected with the dead person. Two-thirds of Murray-Parkes' sample found themselves putting away photographs, and trying to fill their lives with new experiences. However, bereaved people do tend to be occupied by the thoughts of their loss, and are unable to sustain this avoidance. With the passing of time it becomes less necessary to deliberately avoid memories of the lost person.

Anger and guilt. Anger is a normal component of grief, but it changes its form and expression as time passes. During the first month after bereavement anger appears greatest, with a great deal of emotion expressed concerning why the dead person actually died. The people who are most angry are often those who are the most socially isolated. The recognition of the irrationality of their anger leads bereaved people to feel guilty at the way they have behaved.

Freud suggested that individuals frequently experience feelings of ambivalance towards a partner, which gives rise to wish for the other's death. This is tolerable provided it is only a fantasy, but an individual needs a defence against this emotion once the wish has been fulfilled. Thus the bereaved person turns the anger inwards. Naturally, very few relationships are without a certain ambivalance, and Murray-Parkes found a high proportion of guilt due to these feelings in the people he studied.

Gaining a new identity. Part of the process of maturity through bereavement and coming to terms with grief, is the gaining of a new identity. Initially the bereaved person might adopt the values and attitudes of the dead person. This is particularly common if the bereaved person inherits certain of the dead person's roles – for instance, a man who has lost his wife might adopt her attitudes towards child rearing. This becomes less important as the bereaved person grows in confidence and gains a new identity in his/her new role.

Thus bereavement cannot be expressed as a simple stress reaction. It includes psychological and physiological reactions, such as insomnia, anxiety, nervousness, loss of weight and appetite, despair and depression, but it also includes the process by which a person regains a status and role in society. The death of a spouse causes a change in social circumstances due to a process called *stigmatising*. Society is not accustomed to dealing with the bereaved, particularly after the initial shock and the funeral arrangements, so the person suffering is seen as not quite normal or acceptable; they do not fit in. Another source of stress for the recently bereaved is that most married people have pooled financial, emotional and social resources, and so the person who is left alone is without *all* the functions provided by the dead person. During the process of bereavement an individual has to counteract stigmatising and return to 'normality'.

Problems of bereavement

The side-effects of grief and mourning are related to the social disapproval directed against people who cannot join in with everyday life. Although, as Murray-Parkes suggests, grief can be seen as an illness, and is indirectly recognised as such in terms of time taken off work and extra help being provided, the pain of loss for most people extends beyond the normal time allowed for mourning. Many bereaved people feel unable to talk about their memories for a few weeks after the death, by which time friends and relatives are trying to persuade them to take a fresh view of life and look to the future, but mourning will probably not cease until they have been able to express grief and talk about the dead person from the distance that time can provide.

Self-help groups have come into existence over the last few years which enable bereaved people to meet others, compare experiences, and support each other, but it is often necessary for the bereaved person to be able to talk to someone exclusively about their loss, and by doing so set a pattern for re-establishing a life for themselves without the pain or guilt of an unresolved loss. Carole Smith (1982) has reviewed the research studies which looked at the scope for identifying vulnerable individuals and groups, and outlined those responses which may or may not facilitate recovery from the impact of the loss. The issues raised from these studies have led to a consideration of whether professionals should intervene.

Polak *et al.* (1973, cited by Smith, p. 105), and Kincey (1974), found no difference between those people who received help and a control group who did not in terms of their adjustment several months after bereavement. However, Smith cites two other studies (Gerber *et al.*, 1975; Raphael, 1977) which demonstrate that appropriate help given at the time of bereavement and for a period after does facilitate a better outcome for many people than is the case for those who do not receive such help. This corresponds to Murray-Parkes' findings. Smith identifies certain tasks essential to the course of mourning and readjustment (Smith, 1982, p. 110). These are: reorganising the reality of the loss; accepting the reality of the loss; disengaging from the deceased; facing the disruption of reality and meaning; making new relationships and constructing new meanings. The social worker's role is detailed by Smith (pp. 110–24) but it is based upon recognition and identification of the stages and the effective mourning that are part of a psychological reaction to loss.

It is this effective mourning for *any* loss and change which leads to psychological reintegration, which is where social work intervention can help.

Psychological development and gender issues

Life cycle theories such as Erikson's are based upon a model of the *male* life, Richardson (1981) identified the ways in which social work practice favours men, and there would appear to be a direct link between her argument and the fact that practice relies essentially upon theories of male psychology.

Thus:

(1) The literature on working with the elderly frequently stresses retirement and its significance for self-perception. This is primarily a problem for men and is largely irrelevant for understanding women and retirement.

(2) Adolescent sexual behaviour and sexuality are treated differentially. Sexual activity in girls is seen as an indication of pathology and social workers are alerted to 'moral danger' while boys are generally only considered at risk if their sexuality is homosexual.

(3) Traditional ideas of the woman's role in the family still persist. This is particularly true in the area of child welfare, where notions of parental inadequacy have been based on a model of the nuclear family.

(4) The majority of people who receive psychiatric help are women, and in social work the majority of clients are women. This reflects the idea that femininity is pathological (Richardson, 1981).

The subsequent emphasis on community care has meant the woman's role in the family as 'nurturer' is becoming emphasised and extended.

The developing psychology of women attempts to provide a female psychology which is not constructed according to the needs of men. It has taken three routes to this, all of which are relevant here.

Firstly it has reviewed previous psychological data on women's psychology and suggested the source and forms of bias which have filtered into 'common sense' psychology – much of which becomes operationalised by professionals (social workers, health professionals and psychologists). Secondly, it is beginning to develop an explanation of how women's psychology has been constructed as subordinate in a patriarchal context (Hollway, 1989). Thirdly, it has re-evaluated the relationship between female psychology and biology which had been proposed by (mainly) male psychologists. Feminist psychologists have demonstrated the systematic pathologisation of femininity and propose a 'normal' model of female psychology (Nicolson, 1988; Ussher, 1989).

Traditional psychological views of femininity

Apart from Freud's view that femininity is a repressed condition (for discussion see Mitchell, 1974; Sayers, 1982), there is a tradition in academic psychology which conceptualises women as pathological and inadequate. Studies in the 1970s attempted to expose this and demonstrate the effects upon women themselves.

The underlying theme is that well-adjusted women are those whose behaviour and personality centre on mothering/nurturing in the family and their working lives. Femininity was equated with passivity and dependence and one study demonstrated that clinicians of both sexes rated such characteristics as less mature, less healthy and less socially competent than the stereotypical description of masculinity – i.e. independent, assertive and so on. The more 'masculine' a man, the more likely he is seen to have achieved positive mental health, the more 'feminine' a woman, the less likely she is seen to have done the same (Broverman *et al.*, 1970). This paradoxical view permeates traditional psychological assumptions even in the face of contradictory eveidence. For instance, that women are less likely than men to seek re-marriage after widowhood or divorce as they can cope independently (Bernard, 1976).

Women therefore often resist being successful and independent and demonstrate a 'motive to avoid success' (Horner, 1974) with the intention of making themselves socially acceptable. This is then reflected in low self-esteem among women (Williams, 1974).

The construction of female psychology

Research inspired by feminist psychology has tackled these issues, without attributing the 'problem' to women. Instead, the emphasis has been to examine the *social processes* which contribute to the construction of female psychology.

The argument is that psychological knowledge is produced and reproduced from within specific historical conditions and power relations so that existing gender/power relations come to be taken as somehow 'natural' rather than the direct result of ideology (Leonard, 1984; Hollway, 1989).

The 'raging hormone' theory

One means of pathologising women has been to suggest their very biology has negative effects on their competence. For example it is argued that both the pre-menstrual syndrome and post-natal depression may result in women being out of control, so that on occasions they are judged innocent (or incompetent) of serious crimes such as murder, or less serious offences, such as road accidents as they are deemed to be 'ill' with PMS or PND.

Less dramatically, women expect and are expected to perform less well pre-menstrually. Recent research evidence however, has demonstrated quite clearly that this is not so (Richardson, 1987; Sommer, 1987; Ussher, 1989). Further it has been shown that far from hormone changes after birth producing depression, it is likely that the stress of birth and maternal isolation are likely to precipitate depression (Elliot, 1985) and that this is a normal response to such events. Indeed childbirth and early motherhood may be better understood as a 'loss' of time, personal space, relationship patterns, figure and health, and that depression is a normal part of a 'grief' reaction to be encouraged rather than seen as pathological (Nicolson, 1988). (See earlier in this chapter for a discussion of grief.)

Conclusions

The psychology of human development represents an important contribution towards social work knowledge. It needs to be taught and explained in an integrated way so that social workers come to understand the nature of developmental processes, and the ways they occur at various stages of life.

Psychological research on moral development and reasoning suggests that 'right' and 'wrong' are complex issues, and practitioners need to take psychological as well as legal dimensions into account.

The loss and change model of development is also complex, but attempts to integrate psychological biography and social context in trying to understand individual behaviour.

The psychology of women and women's development is a key area for social workers as developmental psychology has hitherto been explained via the model which is based on the male life cycle, and women's position is explained only after priority is given to that of men.

Social workers and their clients are often women and need this perspective to make sense of their own lives and those of their clients. Social workers who are not women also need to have a value-free version of psychology for similar reasons.

7

Social Work Settings

Introduction

So far, the main issues raised have concentrated upon social work involvement with clients. However, social workers themselves are subject to the influence of psychological forces in their daily working lives, and in this chapter the focus is upon the application of psychology to understanding and operating within three kinds of social work setting: fieldwork, residential care, and day care.

Staff relationships in fieldwork

Although social work is a highly individual experience for most workers, most fieldwork agencies arrange their staff in teams. Payne, in his extensive analysis of the nature of social work teams (1982, pp. 6–8), has divided the literature into two main theoretical approaches: the *developmental approach*, based upon the assumption that the teams are essentially social groups; and the *contingency approach*, which is more specifically related to the idiosyncrasies of the individuals who comprise the teams and the organisations in which they operate.

The approach adopted in this book relies most heavily on the theory related to social groups, because it seems particularly relevant for social work teams, and because there is already some emphasis on group dynamics in Chapter 4, thus making the optimum use of the theoretical material already introduced.

There are three important aspects of staff relationships in fieldwork for which psychological theory relating to the social psychology of groups is important:

(1) Understanding the importance of the dynamics of the team to its own functioning, and the functioning of the individual worker. Evidence from early work in industrial psychology makes an important contribution in this area, as well as the more sophisticated understanding of group performance which has been developed subsequently.
(2) The notion of 'acceptable behaviour' and conformity by individual social workers to the values and norms imposed by the agency according to policy. (The impact of forces towards conformity and obedience was examined in Chapter 4.)
(3) The processes involved in decision-making groups which are an integral part of the work of social work agencies.

The dynamics of the team

There are three major sources of influence affecting the dynamics of the social work team: group membership; group cohesiveness; and social facilitation.

Group membership. This refers to the nature of the group in terms of how well members relate to one another, share common goals, identify with their colleagues, or whether they merely see themselves as sharing the same office accommodation. Group membership inevitably affects a person's beliefs and activities. As discussed in Chapter 4, groups exert pressure on their members to conform to particular points of view and ways of doing things, and if individuals do not or cannot share the same values as the other members of the group, they are likely to leave or withdraw emotionally. Membership of the team is important, because it is a source of support to workers who are otherwise quite isolated. If this support is not available it will reduce the quality of the service to clients: incompatible and unsatisfying work groups have been shown to be a major source of dissatisfaction to workers, and to adversely affect the quality of their work.

Group cohesiveness. This is the term used by social psychologists to refer to the degree to which members are attracted to one another and the group as a whole. A high degree of attraction between members means that value is placed on group membership, and that group is said to be cohesive. Early studies in industrial psychology were concerned with improving the efficiency and the discipline of the workforce. By the 1930s it had become clear to psychologists that the workplace was a social setting, and that relationships at work were very important. Cohesiveness in a work group was found to benefit the workers in so far as their morale increased and they reported a higher level of job satisfaction.

Although it may be argued that social work itself can be a satisfying occupation, it is extremely stressful for much of the time because many clients are likely to be on the brink of a crisis or experiencing chronic suffering. Cohesive work groups enable workers to cope better with stressful situations. It has been found that in a cohesive group, workers confide in one another, and as a result there is less absenteeism and less job turnover. In terms of dealing with the 'bureaucratic' aspects of social work; it has been shown that in cohesive groups the level and degree of communication is enhanced, making for greater efficiency.

There are, however, forces which prevent groups from becoming cohesive. For example, the more people there are in a team, the more likely it is that only a few will take on responsibility. It is fairly common for teams to include senior practitioners or specialist workers, social work assistants, trainees, unqualified workers and sometimes students on fieldwork placements. As each will be an equal team member on one level, but on another have a different degree of responsibility and power, a hierarchy (both official and unofficial) is likely to form. In an hierarchical structure, attraction and friendship patterns are affected, so there may be problems for a group when junior and senior members are friends: junior staff may see the senior person as patronising, senior members are censured by other senior people for 'fraternising', and may distrust overtures of friendship from junior group members, seeing these as flattery or other attempts at manipulation.

Promotion of individuals within cohesive teams exacerbates these difficulties, and if a team increases its membership it is likely that sub-groups or cliques will form. As we have seen in Chapter 2, groups tend to compete against one another, and membership of one clique increases hostility and suspicion towards another. The existence of cliques is likely to increase secrecy and gossip, reducing the effectiveness of communication. Secrecy may reduce friction, because if knowledge is restricted, those who benefit are less likely to be challenged by those who do not, as they do not know! However, secrecy derogates those from whom the information is kept. Thus large groups are not cohesive.

Group cohesiveness is *increased* by any factor which enhances the value of the group to an individual member, such as success in achieving goals. Outside threats tend to increase the group's value to its members. This is particularly noticeable in the face of cutbacks which have been threatened to the budgets of various social work agencies. The staff become much more united in purpose, and attraction and communication levels are higher.

Individuals working in the presence of others frequently experience an improved level of work from when they work alone. This is referred to as *social facilitation*, and has proved to be universal. Social workers who experience themselves as members of a team, may well work more effectively than if they were unaware of the presence of other team members. This effect was first noted in the 1920s, when it was observed that cyclists who were trying to beat the clock on their own improved their performance when competing against others. Subsequent work by psychologists in the laboratory and in field studies has confirmed that when people perform in the presence of others their own performance improves.

The social facilitation effect has been explained in terms

of higher psychological arousal experienced in the presence of others, and concern with receiving positive or negative reactions to one's performance. But it may be affected most by the *diffusion of responsibility* that often takes place in groups. This occurs on occasions when a group effort is to be evaluated, and a contribution expected from everyone. The output is frequently less than would be expected from individual member's contributions. It has been proposed that some members engage in 'social loafing' and do not contribute much as their efforts will not be recognised as emanating from them. This may be reflected in the consequence of team projects, for example a reorganisation of an intake system, which makes the team rather than the individual worker responsible for the assessment done prior to allocation to individual workers: less work may be put into the assessment than if an individual had sole responsibility.

Conformity and obedience

The degree of pressure to which individual social workers are subject is an important consideration when trying to understand staff relationships in fieldwork. The theory relevant to this is discussed in Chapter 4.

Decision-making in groups

In social work agencies policy decisions are frequently evolved from group decision making. This is certainly the method by which national policies are arrived at. Recently more and more decisions involving social work have come into the province of committees or panels set up to decide, for instance, whether children should be placed on the At-Risk Register, whether adoption or foster placements should be made, and the way in which financial resources should be allocated. Psychologists have been interested in the way in which groups actually reach their decisions, that is the group performance and whether this performance demonstrates a level of group effectiveness: how well the information had been processed, how relevant the decision was to the circumstances. They have demonstrated that certain biases are common in decision-making groups. These relate to:

(1) The predispositions of the individual members. In an ideal group, each member's attitudes, opinions and beliefs would be discussed openly, and evaluated by the group. Each member would try to understand her colleagues, and reach a balanced outcome. Research into decision-making in juries has highlighted the impact that predisposition has upon final voting patterns, and has shown that in many cases, evidence presented after one has made up one's mind has little impact on final voting, despite persuasive discussion.

(2) If a group reaches a minimally acceptable solution to a problem, then group members frequently develop a bias in favour of that solution. So in a committee meeting to consider financial cuts, the solution of reducing the number of administrative staff may be floated, and accepted by the most talkative members. This isolation then becomes the one which group members become biased towards and argue to defend, even though they did not necessarily start out by believing this to be the best solution to the problem. There is a general failure among group members to accept criticisms and new ideas, and researchers have found that this is a widespread pattern in groups solving complex problems, like many of those relevant to social work. The actual processes involved in these cases are that several ideas are put forward until a solution meets with some positive response from the most active members. Once there is a minimal agreement, there is a shift in the quality of the discussion with a search towards justification rather than criticism. If new solutions are offered, it is these that are criticised.

Not only are there biases in decision-making groups, but groups also tend to reach polarised decisions. It has been shown that groups will frequently take *risky* decisions to which individual members themselves are not privately committed. This has been called the 'risky shift' phenomenon. A group of social workers and related professionals might decide to send a child home from residential care to his parents, or decide not to renew a statutory treatment section on a psychiatric patient although privately each individual member of the group might not be prepared to take such a risk alone. Reasons for this might be diffusion of responsibility, or a cultural norm which favours risk, or at least rejects 'over-protectiveness'. Also, group discussions release members from certain inhibitions which they experience when alone. Research into the 'risky shift' effect has also demonstrated that sometimes groups favour decisions which are more conservative than individuals might have made. The main conclusion must be that group decisions tend to be polarised, more extreme than individual members' decisions might be outside the group.

Finally, returning to the effect of cohesiveness in groups, we will focus on the work of Irving Janis. He did research into group decision-making in the late 1960s, when he suggested that cohesive groups are impaired in their effectiveness by 'groupthink'. This occurs when the group's need for consensus overwhelms the members' realistic appraisal of alternative courses of action. Groups of close friends are under a great deal of pressure to agree and do not want to criticise or challenge the ideas of people they like. Janis argues that this may well be disastrous because it limits the number of alternatives, prevents the groups from fully examining the action it is taking and avoids seeking expert opinion to support one particular line of argument against another.

There are thus a great many characteristics of fieldwork teams which affect the nature and quality of individual workers' efforts for their clients, and the way policy and practical decisions are made. Despite the apparently individual nature of fieldwork, it is clearly influenced by group dynamics, and an understanding of these processes is useful for professional survival among social workers.

Staff relationships in residential work

Residential social workers experience different conditions from fieldworkers. They are by definition more involved with their clients' lives and as such experience a great deal of stress. They also come up against much criticism from outside commentators, and are particularly confronted with the accusation that they are instrumental (even if unwittingly) in the process of institutionalisation that their clients suffer. Some interesting and useful studies have been made looking at what staff in residential homes actually do, and the defences they operate in order to alleviate some of the stress.

Residential staff also work as part of a team, and the same dynamics apply to their inter-relationships as to the fieldworkers', but the residential experience is usually a more intensive one, with the emphasis on group development and the effects of organisational stress.

The nature of the residential task

Residential workers in general do not have the opportunity to remove themselves from their clients' lives by doing bureaucratic tasks, as do fieldworkers. Residential work involves constant confrontation with clients' needs and problems and very often the workers see themselves as the cause of some of these problems. Some studies have made significant contributions towards understanding how residential workers deal with these immediately stressful situations. They have been based on the hypothesis proposed by Elliot Jaques concerning *social defence systems*, which has been developed from the psychoanalytic approach to psychology outlined in Chapter 1.

Jaques considered that in an organisation the defence against anxiety is one of the primary elements which bind individuals together. In other words, he suggested that within an organisation maladaptive behaviours such as hostility and suspicion will be exhibited, and these are the social counterparts of the symptoms that an individual might exhibit through projection (a concept in psycho-dynamic theory dealt with in Chapter 1, a defence mechanism which occurs when someone attributes to another person a characteristic which is in fact their own). Thus Jaques sees individuals as externalising impulses which would otherwise give rise to anxiety, and 'pooling' them in the life of the social institutions in which they associate.

To illustrate this more clearly, it is worth quoting from some research undertaken at a teaching hospital (Menzies, 1970). This was a study of the way that nurses cope, or fail to cope, with their job, but is relevant to residential workers. Menzies found that the nurses in her study experienced a great deal of anxiety, and set out to understand how they managed to tolerate it. She found that there were two mechanisms for dealing with anxiety: the personal and the institutional.

Individual nurses, by the nature of their jobs, were faced with coping with stress and emotions surrounding the physical care of patients, comforting relatives, comforting patients who were sometimes hostile, and having intimate contact with patients that they might find distressing or even repugnant. In addition, patients and relatives experienced a great many conflicting emotions concerning the nurses: gratitude for the care and attention, envy of their skills and health, and hostility because of their forced dependence. Menzies claims that the nurses project their anxieties into their work situation; because this was unsupportive the nurses were unable to develop coping mechanisms, and so they regressed. This was exacerbated by the 'social defence system' of the organisation, which is the result of each member of the nursing staff's collusion as they operate their own defence mechanisms.

Menzies provides several examples to explain and illustrate this. One of the most important is the way the nurses attempted to minimise their anxiety regarding individual responsibility. Each nurse experienced a powerful internal conflict between the responsibility demanded by her work, and her wishes to avoid this heavy and continuous burden of acting responsibly. This conflict was partially avoided by the processes of splitting, denial and projection, which converted this intra-personal struggle into an inter-personal one. In Menzies' words: 'Each nurse tends to split off aspects of herself from her conscious personality, and to project them into other nurses'. Thus the irresponsible impulses were split off and projected into a nurse's subordinate, who was then treated with the severity which that part of the split-off self deserved. The stern and harsh aspects of herself were split-off and projected onto her superiors so that she expected harsh disciplinary treatment from them. It could be observed that nurses frequently claimed that other nurses were careless, irresponsible and in need of continual supervision and discipline.

Defences against anxiety are also defences against reality, when situations become too stressful to bear. However, operating defence system like the ones that Menzies described requires energy which is deflected from the primary task of caring for the inmates of the institution. Thus residential staff may actually become 'institutionalised' themselves, a phenomenon which is frequently observed. This means that they are less open to new ideas, less responsive to individual needs, and unlikely to create an environment which enables the residents to operate as individuals.

Miller and Gwynne (1972), in their study of residential institutions for the physically handicapped and young chronic sick, used a similar theoretical base. They looked at the primary task of the institution and concluded that society assigns the staff the task of catering for the 'socially dead' during the interval between social death and physical death. When people cross the boundary into such an institution, they show that they have failed to occupy or retain any role which, according to the norms of society, confers social status on the individual. However, most staff do not consider the notion of social death as significant, probably because it is too painful. The staff are there because of advances in medicine, prolonging life of the chronically sick and disabled, because families are no longer equipped to cope with handicapped members and because of cultural changes in society which have deprived it of adequate cultural mechanisms for coping with death. In contemporary society, death is frequently considered obscene, although this is probably slowly changing. Most residential staff in long-stay institutions are committed to caring and probably see themselves as taking on a task with which most people are unable to cope. Miller and Gwynne demonstrate that there are two models of defence systems which these staff might operate:

The humanitarian defence. Despite social death, there is a pressure of humanitarian values to ensure that the interval between social and physical death is as long as possible: sick people in old people's homes are given medical treatment, even if their life will be reduced in quality afterwards, and staff are not prepared to hear the residents' complaints about their lack of fulfilment and unhappiness, or their wishes to die. This is seen as an affront to humanitarian values.

The liberal defence. Superficially the liberal defence is at odds with the humanitarian defence. The abnormalities of the inmates is denied, and hopes of physical and social rehabilitation are encouraged. However, the truth is soon realised by those inmates who venture back across the boundary and find they do not easily fit into 'normal' society. Miller and Gwynne found that staff who profess liberal values also tend to 'infantalise' their inmates by claiming they are really normal, but in much the way that babies and children are: they refer to the inmates' activities in a patronising way, realising that they are not normal, but refusing to admit it openly.

Goffman, in his work on psychiatric institutions, draws attention to the fact that staff have roles and statuses which are not only recognised internally, but have external meaning: they are not only in the institution to serve the needs of the inmates, and serve society by providing care for its rejects, but are often there to gain professional experience in order to move on to other positions. This is another way individual staff can prevent themselves from becoming overwhelmed by the suffering of the people in their care.

Residential workers, then, appear to face an impossible task, made worse by their own staff and professional networks seeming to deny the reality of the anxiety this type of work produces. In the next section, the *therapeutic community* model of residential care will be developed. This goes some way towards enabling staff to support one another while being aware of the reality of the work they are doing.

Residential and day care from the clients' perspective

There are a variety of factors in residential and day care which inhibit or encourage emotional development in clients for whom they are provided. The physical facilities and resources are an obvious influence on the scope of the experience, but probably more significant are the attitudes and behaviour of the staff.

The problematic relationships faced by the staff are experienced at first hand by the clients. The extremes of regime which are possible greatly affect the quality of life experienced by the client. The different models of residential and day care, and their effects, will be discussed in this section. If we are to accept Miller and Gwynne's notion of 'social death', then it can be applied to a greater or lesser extent to most residential and day care institutions. Certainly, people attending day nurseries and luncheon clubs are still very much part of the wider society, but there is also evidence that children in residential care suffer permanent emotional damage from their experiences. It is not 'social death' in the sense of being a state of suspension between being a full member of society and being physically dead, but it does *impair* all these individuals' capacity to live.

This impairment may be in the form of 'institutional neurosis' as described by Barton (1976). He showed how people who spend a long period in psychiatric hospital adopt certain bizarre characteristics such as strange ways of walking, a lack of interest in their surroundings and a general mood of passivity; all of these to a greater or lesser extent can be seen in clients for whom attending a day centre is the main focus of their lives, or who live permanently or temporarily in institutions. This is true for children, but studies in residential nurseries have shown a retardation effect in learning and a lack of facility for forming relationships. Reports of older children in residential institutions have demonstrated passivity and dependence in addition to an inability to form lasting relationships.

Models of institutions

Miller and Gwynne describe two models of residential care which correspond with the humanitarian and liberal values previously described. They call these models the 'warehousing model' and the 'horticultural model'. In the warehousing model, the primary task is to prolong physical life, and it translates the model of the hospital into the setting of the residential home. The new resident is defined in terms of physical malfunctioning and is provided with medical and nursing care. The horticultural model caters for an inmate who is perceived as deprived, with unsatisfied drives and unfulfilled capacities. The primary task of the institution is to develop these capacities. The staff provide the residents with opportunities for growth. Miller and Gwynne admit that the horticultural model is an aspiration rather than a reality.

Therapeutic communities

The development of the therapeutic community actually made some inroads into tackling the problems of institutionalisation and dependence. The original therapeutic community was the Social Rehabilitation Unit in Surrey, which is now known as the Henderson. It originally catered for ex-prisoners of war who were unable to maintain themselves in society because of social inadequacies. Maxwell Jones, who was the medical superintendent of the unit, felt that the *social relationships* of these people needed to be developed, rather than that they should receive medical treatment. He involved staff and residents in the task of providing social feedback on how each of them coped with their work and social routines, which were part of a strict regime.

The therapeutic community model developed by Jones enabled all staff and residents to participate in treatment and policy making. The 'therapeutic' component was related to rehabilitation to a role in society which was the primary aim, via the 'community', which was the sum of all the people who lived and worked there. The hierarchy was flattened, and responsibility diffused, and thus a sense of community or joint decision-making could arise. In this model everyone is aware of what is happening to everyone else, and is free to comment accordingly. A 'twenty-four hour living learning experience' is what Jones claimed for this approach, and it meant that all interactions between community members had therapeutic potential. The therapeutic community represents a social microcosm, a miniature society, where individuals can practise new roles, and be made aware of their social and interpersonal impact. Residents also had adminstrative responsibility. All this was done through a rigid network of policy and psychotherapeutic groups, which everyone had to attend, and where they exposed themselves to situations from which they could receive feedback on their behaviour.

This is a very stressful approach for staff and residents, but does prevent passivity and apathy, and makes people aware of their potential and ability to contribute to their own and other people's treatment. This mechanism is called *sociotherapy* and involves the treatment and reinforcement of a person's ability to perform roles within the microcosmic society. it is of course difficult to provide any kind of therapy or treatment which does not include an element of coercion, because by definition the person who needs therapy does so in order to be accepted by society, and this only happens if a deviant learns to conform. However, it is the broader use of this model which is of most concern to social workers.

Wider applications of the therapeutic community approach

It has been suggested that there is a difference between the therapeutic community proper, and the therapeutic community *approach*. The Henderson represents the therapeutic community proper, but other institutions can adopt the important characteristics such as regular group meetings, and a flattening of the hierarchy. It is the opportunity to participate in community decisions, and provide feedback on people's behaviour, that enables most experiences of dependence and passivity to be reversed. Powerful hierarchies can only exist if communication and information are exclusive to particular groups of people. The opening of information provides fairly rapid changes in the nature of institutions.

Martin (1962), describing the therapeutic community approach as it was introduced to a ward of long-stay female psychiatric patients, records how many of the nurses and junior doctors resisted the move to redistribute power. However, the most striking demonstration in his work is the change in the behaviour and emotional responses of the women who had been 'written off' by society. They had developed an interest in their fate and surroundings in the course of a few months.

Adult day centres and residential institutions offer much scope for sociotherapy to be introduced, and indeed this has been done in a variety of settings. The psychiatric profession has neglected to make use of the model, but on the whole social work agencies are more flexible and keen to find ways of improving their clients' experiences of life. The basis of this model is that it is not the individual in need of treatment so much, but the residential or day care setting itself, which is in need of change. The only change that is to the advantage of the clients is one which enables them to express their opinions and views and have them acted on where appropriate.

Work with children presents conceptual difficulties as well as practical ones. Statutory limitations impose restrictions on the degree of democracy which can be introduced in institutions for children, but it is still possible for children to be informed of the circumstances surrounding their lives in care, the fate of the other children they are living with, and to have an equal say in decisions crucial to their own lives. Naturally the aims and objectives of residential and day care settings vary, but most would achieve at least some of their aims by increasing the emphasis on sociotherapy, which entails the use of all the client's experiences in assisting emotional growth.

8

Social Policy, Social Work and Psychology

Research in psychology (as in any other discipline) is constrained by *political* decisions about 'what we need to know'. So for instance in the late 1980s, medical and psychological research has been focused on the treatment, sexual and social behaviour of AIDS victims, and child sexual abuse has also attracted funds for research (La Fontaine, 1989).

Psychologists and social workers themselves select from the scientific knowledge available, so that when knowledge has also been pre-selected according to politically deemed need, it is crucial that practitioners exercise caution in evaluating and applying this knowledge.

In this chapter we want to examine the influence that social policy has had upon what appears to be 'objective' psychological knowledge which has noticeably informed social work practice.

We want to look firstly at the relationship between social policy and notions of 'good' child-care practice, apparently based on psychological knowledge. Then we want to examine the relationship between community care initiatives and psychological knowledge (see Griffiths, 1988).

Psychology and child-care practice

Modern child-care policy had its origins in the late 1940s with the creation of the Children's Departments. Over the last 30 to 40 years ideas of 'what is best' for children have fluctuated and may have come full circle. There is sometimes an unfortunate interrelationship between the advice of 'experts' and the results of tragic incidents such as the death of Maria Colwell, a victim of a policy which supported the view that children should be with the natural parent regardless of the emotional and physical cost. Such attitudes are based upon a misconception of the validity of certain components of psychological knowledge. It had been understood (and often still is) that women have a 'maternal instinct' which propels them towards motherhood and makes them protect their offspring even at the risk of their own lives. Such a view was economically and politically expedient (as we shall see later in this chapter) but with no scientific basis.

Badinter (1980) clearly demonstrates through an historical analysis of motherhood in France that mothering is a political rather than instinctual form of behaviour. This debate provides vital evidence for social workers. The non-existence of a 'maternal instinct' does not suggest that women do not and cannot behave in nurturing ways; it simply means that ideology, culture and economic context are more important predictors of the quality of parental care a child is likely to receive.

Since the 1975 Children Act, children's needs have been assessed on a more individual basis, with safety issues overriding 'psychological' ones. In 1948, as a result of the Curtis report, the children's department came into being. This was eventually incorporated into the social services department after 1970. Jean Packman (1975) has written a detailed account of the social, economic and psychological influences which informed committees of inquiry from Curtis to Houghton (whose recommendation resulted in the 1975 Children Act). She described child-care policy since 1948 as demonstrating:

> The constraints and opportunities of a legal framework; the interaction between central and local government; the influence of practitioners as well as official 'policy makers'; the effect – or lack of it – of research, pressure groups and scandals; the circular relationship between

needs and demands and service responses; and the vital, sometimes fraught and sometimes fruitful partnership between local government officers and their council members.

In this section, the importance of psychological concepts and research will be demonstrated in relation to the framing of this policy; also the ways in which contrasting decisions about priorities in child-care were related to the political climate, but justified in terms of psychological 'fact'. This will be shown by four examples illustrated from evolutionary stages in child-care policy. These are:

(1) The notion of substitute care will be examined in the context of the choice of foster homes over residential children's homes.
(2) The justification for maintaining the child's stable relationship with the natural parents will be considered against the benefits of substitute families.
(3) The case for adoption in preference to preventive casework.
(4) The delinquent's needs for care and treatment contrasted with the need for strict discipline and the 'short sharp shock' as a deterrent for juvenile crime.

Foster homes v. residential care

From the mid to the late 1940s, several factors indicated that the piecemeal provision for underprivileged children was inadequate. The Monckton Inquiry of 1945 into the death of Dennis O'Neill after mistreatment in a foster home focused on:

(1) problems in *administering* the 'boarding-out' or fostering service;
(2) the initial selection of suitable foster homes.

The Curtis Committee, whose report resulted in the establishment of an integrated child-care service, focused upon the poor quality of the residential child-care institutions. The main function of the new children's department was to find suitable foster homes for 'deprived' children, with the aim of providing, via the foster family, a better set of social relationships, a good experience of family life and a variety of human contacts for the child. There was also to be an emphasis upon emptying the orphanages of all the children who were unlikely to return to their parents.

There were various psychological research reports which suggested that institutional care from infancy was likely to result in retardation of cognitive skills and intellectual development, as well as impaired emotional growth (e.g. Spitz, 1945). The Curtis Committee itself presented evidence that children in foster homes seemed to be more integrated into society than children in orphanages who experienced the effects of segregation. Curtis reported that children in foster homes were less starved of affection and more independent than those in residential care. These findings were given extra significance by evidence from the work of John Bowlby. He produced a report for the World Health Organisation (1951) apparently demonstrating that children brought up in institutions were much more likely to suffer disturbed emotional and intellectual development than those who were in a family. In addition, fostercare had one great political advantage over residential care – it was very cheap. It was a generally held belief that substitute care for children was provided for love rather than money, and that high rates of pay for foster parents were closely linked with child exploitation, so payments to foster parents were kept low. In the early 1950s there was a great deal of pressure on the number of children's departments to save money on the number of children they had in care in England and Wales, which had increased by 10 000 between 1949 and 1953. Therefore an economic solution had to be provided, and this tied in with current psychological evidence that institutional care was damaging.

Even so, the rationale for this development of foster care was based mainly on the research evidence related to the *negative effects of residential institutions*, and not so much on the benefits of foster care. It was also clear that improving residential care would cost much more than increasing the supply of foster homes, and so no evidence on how institutional care might be improved, or even be of ultimate benefit to children, was presented. This resulted in the decline of the children's home: residential staff received less money and training, and recruitment in this area declined in quantity and quality. Some time later, in 1963, the Williams Committee found that only 15 per cent of staff in local authority children's homes were qualified. Field-workers had much higher status, and morale among residential staff dropped. It has remained so with all but a few exceptions. (See below for Barclay's recommendations for residential and day-care staff.)

Sociological and psychological research has examined a variety of institutions and demonstrated ways in which a process of 'institutionalisation' occurs for residential workers and inmates. This is characterised by flattened emotional responses, retarded learning, poor memory, and conformity. Thus instutitional life is considered undesirable. However, it is within the realms of most social scientists' imaginations to see that a residential experience might provide opportunities that family life cannot, in terms of adaptability to a variety of social relationships, understanding the implications of living with other people, reducing desire to compete and seek attention, and other socially-oriented characteristics. (This argument was developed briefly in Chapter 7 and is also proposed by Lee and Pithers in 'Radical Social Work and Practice', 1980.) The introduction of these points in this context is to demonstrate that social policy is not value-free in the way it selects psychological evidence to support decisions; and that the major impetus behind the expansion of fostering is more likely to have been economic than a result of psychological research.

Preventive casework

Although fostering as a form of substitute care has never been totally neglected, the children's department did find it difficult to match all the children in need to suitable foster homes. The task was becoming a burden, and so they responded by seeking alternatives which were equally cheap. Such alternatives had been discussed as early as 1946 by the Women's Group on Public Welfare (a subcommittee of Curtis) which had looked at 'The Neglected Child and His Family'. They argued that the removal of a child from his family was an easy answer to an unsatisfactory home, but not psychologically sound in terms of the child's emotional life. They proposed the radical suggestion that an 'intensive family casework service' might provide ways of helping families stay together. This of course is well supported by Bowlby's thesis that continuous care, preferably from the child's mother, is best for his future mental health. Thus child-care officers were trained in 'preventive' work, but there was also a need for legislation to enable them to intervene in a family if they were not going to remove a child. This came in the form of the 1952 Children and Young Persons (Amendment) Act, which gave local authorities the right to enter the homes of children who were likely to be at risk of going into care. This was justified by the psychological concept that *separation from the natural parent increases a child's deprivation*. It was also becoming apparent that children suffering from neglect often had parents with similar backgrounds. Local authorities found themselves intervening in families where adequate emotional and physical care could not be provided, and in doing so were likely to reinforce the family's inadequacy, and do nothing to prevent its effects on subsequent generations.

Those who advocated 'preventive casework' were of the opinion that if financial pressures were reduced, then casework might enable families to modify their existing capacities for relationships and provide a suitable environment for child-care. Thus, in the 1963 Children Act, the local authorities were empowered to provide material and monetary aid for families, which was important since the National Assistance Board was frequently too inflexible to provide additional help for deprived families. The implementation of this Act meant that more children were supervised at home than were received into care, and it increased the complexity and workload of the children's department once again. The child-care officer was not in a position to weigh the dangers of *separation* for children against the *physical, material or emotional* neglect they might be suffering, and be equipped with a variety of possible solutions. However, statistics show that the emphasis in this period was on *prevention* which reflects the policy of the era rather than a 'value-free' assessment.

Permanent substitute care

The link between the natural parents and the child was challenged ten years later in the light of events which once again affected policy development. In 1971, the Seebohm Committee's recommendations resulted in the social services departments being formed from existing welfare services. Shortly afterwards the death of Maria Colwell, who had been returned to her mother from foster parents by social workers, resulted in the Houghton Committee Inquiry. The report expressed concern for children who were suffering because bonds with their natural parents were being preserved at all costs.

A report from the National Children's Bureau highlighted the vulnerability of children who were 'born to fail' because of their social and economic background, and contrasted their prospects with those of children from similar backgrounds who had been adopted. Barbara Tizard's work *Adoption: A Second Chance* (1975) presents case studies of children who had overcome earlier deprivations due to the security achieved by living with permanent substitute families. Tizard argues that security and love are more important to children's welfare than being with the natural parent when they cannot provide this.

The 1975 Children Act emphasised the need to protect the *child's* interests above all others especially when they are in conflict with the needs and desires of the natural parents. BASW refers to this as the 'adversary model' and rightly expressed the fear that changes in legislation to this effect could well ignore the subtleties in attachments between parents and children. Parents would be discouraged from requesting voluntary receptions into care because they feared that admitting the need for help with child-care might expose them to the possible permanent loss of their children. The Children Act, of course, gave increased powers to social workers to make decisions about what actions would be in the child's best interests.

Social workers over recent years have also evolved a more specialist service for children. This is as a result of the inadequacies highlighted by inquiries into cases of child abuse, and the frustration many social workers have felt in not being able to 'specialise'. The new specialist services have included social workers and social work teams with responsibility for child sexual abuse, non-accidental injury, and specialist fostering and adoption workers.

Juvenile delinquency

Children's departments were not primarily concerned with delinquency. This remained the province of the Home Office until the 1960s. In 1956 the report of the Ingleby Inquiry which focused upon the power of the juvenile courts and residential treatment facilities for children, gave evidence that the children who came before the courts did so because they had been exposed to cruelty, neglect and danger. They linked neglect and ill-treatment of children to the incidence of juvenile delinquency, and this gave rise to a series of reports and White Papers during the 1960s. Delinquency had been rising, and although this was previously blamed on wartime upheaval and separation of evacuees from parents, this no longer held true. The growing body of opinion was that prevention of distress in children would prevent deviant behaviour. It was also clear that the type of institution (the approved school) to which young offenders were sent was not having the reforming effect that was hoped.

The Children and Young Persons Act (1969) saw the delinquent as a victim of circumstances whose offence was a cry for help, and therefore care and treatment should be provided to meet this need. This was in the form of community homes with education, which were set up to deal with most delinquents committed to care. Under this Act the social worker was able to place a child in care at home. The magistates were empowered to command the care order, but had no say in the placement. Also, social workers could supervise children at home under a Supervision Order, and there was the possibility of Intermediate Treatment being included in this. This provided a sentencing option for magistrates and a duty was placed on local authorities to make money available for preventive work with young offenders. For many local authorities though, this has only recently been exploited on a large scale.

The liberalism of the 1960s and 1970s declined in the light of the apparent failure of the community homes to curtail delinquency. The present Conservative Government has seen delinquency in terms of criminal behaviour and chosen, as far as possible, to return power to the magistrates and implement more custodial sentences in detention centres and borstals, with the idea that the 'short sharp shock' will solve society's problems. The child's problems are currently of little political interest.

John Bowlby and day nurseries

Tizard and other writers have drawn attention to Bowlby's work, which has probably been the most influential research on child welfare. It also demonstrates in a variety of ways how effectively research findings can be used by politicians to change people's behaviour. Certain aspects of Bowlby's work have been mentioned in Chapter 6 (attachment) and in this chapter, in terms of evidence about the quality of residential institutions. For social workers and their clients the consequences have been a fundamental influence upon a whole generation's (and possibly the subsequent generation's) attitudes, behaviour and provision regarding childcare.

Basically, Bowlby (a psychoanalytically-oriented psychiatrist) argued that the mental health of infants and young children was dependent upon the experience of a warm, intimate and continuous relationship with their mother, or a permanent mother substitute. 'Maternal deprivation' resulted in delinquent, psychopathic or at the very least grave, personality disorders. Bowlby's evidence was gained from studies of residential institutions, hospitals and case studies of children who experienced separation due to wartime evacuation. Some of his work was retrospective, based on work with disturbed children for whom he traced a link with inadequate maternal bonding. His findings were supported by other studies, which looked at emotional deprivation in children in French orphanages.

Despite the source of his evidence, derived from institutions which generally made inadequate provision for the emotional development of children in their care, the conclusion drawn by Bowlby and others from his work was the *separation of a young child from its mother was in itself a bad thing*. Tizard contends that such was the impact of Bowlby's work that this notion almost assumed the status of a *law* in psychology. As such it was not only used in argument against residential care, but for closing day-nurseries, despite the fact that no studies showing deleterious effects of day-nursery placement had been published.

It is now common knowledge that Bowlby's work was used after the Second World War to encourage women who had taken essential jobs in factories as part of the war effort to relinquish them to returning men. They were persuaded of the permanent damage that their children would suffer if they did not offer them fulltime care. The American film (*Rosie the Riveter*) illustrated this dramatically by contrasting the pre war propaganda shown to American mothers about the *benefits* of day-care for their children, with subsequent campaigns telling them of their selfishness, cruelty and maladaptive sexuality if they had not returned to their 'natural' role as fulltime mother.

Shortly after the publication of Bowlby's findings and their recommendations being implemented, other studies like those of Schaffer and Emerson (discussed in Chapter 6) showed that children were capable of forming multiple attachments by the age of 6 months. Subsequent work by psychologists has shown that a child will benefit from forming several attachments, and their social skills in this actually improved with practice. It is only in the 1970s that psychologists have concentrated on the *benefits* of multiple attachments and the lack of such research has been a consequence of the massive political impact of the earlier work. Eckerman and Whatley (1977) have shown the importance of the peer group for emotional and intellectual development. They demonstrated that 10 to 12 month old children will play with each other, and although no *attachment* appears to form, they are not indifferent to their peers. Mueller and Brenner (1977) emphasise the importance of practice in social relationships in 1 to 2 year olds, and Hartup (1970) has shown that 3 year olds and above have 'best friends'. However this whole area has been relatively neglected, and work is currently being encouraged in the USA, where experimental day-nurseries have been set up in conjunction with research projects.

Also in the 1970s, work was done to see whether there was evidence that children at day-nurseries do suffer from 'maternal deprivation'. Willis and Ricutti (1974) studied infants' (4 to 15 months of age) arrivals at day-nursery over a period of 6 months. Most babies greeted the nurses with pleasure, or without distress, and at the end of the day greeted their parents happily. Although Ricutti concluded that children preferred their mother, they had also developed an attachment to the nursery worker. These studies, if taken seriously, go some way to avoiding the blind acceptance of research findings as 'psychological facts'.

Other research in the same period has demonstrated that it may well be damaging for some children to have a close and continuous relationship with one person. It is likely that the child will suffer in some way from the problems that the person experiences, and in the case of depressed mothers the children's accident rate was four times higher than that of children whose mothers were not depressed. Mothers in this study reported loss of interest in their children when they were depressed and anxious. Richman (1976) also found a link between the state of the mother and the child. Mothers who were depressed were most likely to have children with behaviour problems. She asserts that even if they do not exhibit problems, they are less likely to be stimulated by a depressed mother.

Despite a wealth of evidence, which has at least equal if not more validation than Bowlby's work, the research on the benefits for children and parents of day-care has not been incorporated into practice. This is likely to be at least partly related to high rates of unemployment among the male population and the fear that if free from fulltime child-care, women will flood the job market. Tizard has said that the situation will not change until psychologists are taught about 'problem-oriented' psychology, and thus understand that their discipline is not value-free but responsive to social and political pressure. Belskey and Steinberg have stressed the need for psychologists working in the area of day-care for children to ask questions about the impact on parents, families and the social structure. Social workers however, *are* aware of the social and political context of their work, and it is essential that they bring this knowledge into use in any assessment of psychological aspects of their clients' lives and their own role.

Decentralisation of social work: the use of community resources

The past forty years have seen the growth and development of the profession of social work. However within this profession various developmental 'sub-phases' have occurred which demanded reorientations of approach among social workers. These have been in reaction to social policy and economic changes, but have had an impact on the attitudes of social workers towards the use of psychological theory.

The first sub-phase was the professional development with the emphasis on psychodynamic work and social casework. This was followed by the 'sociological' reaction and the growth of community work in the late 1960s and early 1970s, accompanied by a 'flirtation' with the systems approach, requiring that social workers try and make some sense of social institutions as well as of the behaviour of their clients. More recently, social workers have responded to the limitations in their resources and have stressed task-centred and intake work, and crisis intervention. These are relatively cheap ways of dealing with the more demanding problems, but the emphasis on expediency has frequently meant that a consideration of the social causes of individual or family problems has received less time and attention than it deserved. This sub-phase, occurring at the end of the 1970s, appeared at the stage when voluntary agencies, particularly those concerned with community work and prevention, were on the decline. They were classed as agents of 'radical' social work and certain local authorities put forward strong cases for withdrawing any resources they had invested in such projects.

The conservatism of the 1980s has stressed community care, and encouraged the role of volunteers in keeping many people out of institutional care, for economic reasons. Although it was not the overt aim of policy, it set the scene for social workers to think once again in terms of working on a community basis, and many local authorities reorganised their area teams to a patch structure and set up sub-offices.

In 1982 the working party set up by the National Institute of Social Work (Barclay Committee) to review the role and tasks of social workers in social services departments and related voluntary agencies published its report. This report reinforced the trend, stressing the importance of mobilising community resources and informal care. In addition to an emphasis on caring for people in the community it proposed the idea that community social work could be put into practice by using residential and day-care institutions as community resource centres. There have been several examples of this but as yet no formal research into the psychological effects on residents and their relatives. So, for example, some elderly people's homes have become day-centres and clubs as well, and friendships have developed between residents and club members, breaking down social isolation on both sides. Children's community homes have run clubs for old people and handicapped children, encouraging children with social problems, and often a history of delinquency, to do voluntary work and take an interest in various community activities.

Another effect proposed by Barclay is the breaking down of the rigid distinction between field and residential workers, because residential and day-care establishments are proposed as the focus of most of the community-oriented social work, and there is a requirement for all social workers to develop new skills and assess the needs of clients according to very different criteria, which will probably differ from the criteria operated by existing community workers.

The brief outline above, which categorised community work with 'radical sociological' social work was deliberately emphasised. In 1976 the Association of Community Workers stated that 'conventional individual and social psychology offers little help to community workers who work with a range of "normal" individuals . . . in a variety of roles'. They criticise social psychology not only for its *content* (e.g. effects of the mass media, effects of collective action) but also because little work has been done in 'natural' settings. That is, they feel that on the one hand psychological knowledge is irrelevant and should be seen as part of 'psychological studies' and not real life, and on the other hand they feel that psychologists should do some research into what actually happens in communities. This typifies the confusion of 'radicals' who operated in a climate where psychology had not been usefully or critically incorporated into social and community work education, but seen as an outmoded and reactionary discipline.

More recent writers (e.g. Twelvetrees, 1982) have progressed beyond this stance. He encourages the integration of literature on group behaviour and social groupwork into community work theory, stressing that some understanding of group processes will enable the community workers to know what to look for and how to understand what is going on, and so provide an acceptable basis for intervention. He also emphasises the point made by Goetschius that it is important for the worker to help the community group to evaluate its work, and decide how to alter its behaviour and avoid repeating mistakes. Again, Twelvetrees correctly considers that despite the emphasis on action and social change, individual members of community groups suffer from a variety of emotional and psychological reactions. It is important for workers to make sense of these as part of the helping role. It is no longer 'reactionary' to understand the emotional side of people's lives.

So the most recent policy proposals on the future of social work require that social workers extend their practice beyond concern for interpersonal relationships. Psychological theory incorporated into social work training and practice has to be developed and understood accordingly, taking political and sociological perspectives into account. This means that social workers will need to be familiar with *more* psychology, with an increased critical facility to select and integrate relevant knowledge and skills.

Conclusions

Psychology and social work are unable to operate as 'value-free' disciplines. Not only are various groups within society influenced by policy, but researchers and practitioners are greatly affected by the context in which they work. This means that professional practitioners need to reach beyond just the theory; they have to make sense of the origins and context of the whole operation of social work practice. To analyse, understand and continue to practise is often difficult, but it is more problematic in the long term if practitioners attempt to operate in a vacuum.

9

The Future of Psychology and Social Work

The future of psychology and social work is likely to be contentious. There are four reasons for this:

(1) The tensions between the content and knowledge base of the disciplines of psychology and social work.
(2) Substantive changes in social work theory, training and practice.
(3) Substantive changes in psychology.
(4) The effects of these tensions and changes in both disciplines.

Professional psychologists seem determined to (re-)claim some of the ground over which social workers hold sovereignty – for instance, domestic violence, sexual abuse and a range of issues of interest to the new breed of 'counselling psychologists', such as family work, grief counselling and so on. Conversely, some writers (e.g. Howe, 1987) are beginning to 'leapfrog' from principles of nineteenth-century behaviourism to modern social work theory ignoring the ways in which psychological research has refined and applied this knowledge.

In the first edition we indicated Sutton's (1981) recognition that CCETSW (Central Council for Education and Training in Social Work), in the guidelines for social work training courses, requires that social work students have to demonstrate knowledge and understanding of

162

a) Social work theories including their practice in work with individuals, groups and communities and in field, residential and day services; and
b) processes of human development, socialisation and functioning, both normal and deviant, throughout the life cycle, within a multicultural society; the nature of moral behaviour . . .

However, CCETSW does not state that these theories are psychological or derived from psychology – it appears to make the assumption that they are an intrinsic part of social work practice and theory.

This has now become more explicit in what appears to be a denial of psychologists' contribution to social work theory. So from both sides, there are indications of unclear boundaries compounded by both professions engaged in a continual process of reflection and self-scrutiny.

Social work training is slowly being extended (the proposed Qualifying Diploma in Social Work QDSW) and more broadly grounded in practice, but continues to demand a high academic standard including psychological knowledge (CCETSW, 1988).

Psychology in Britain (following the USA) has engaged in a study of the future of the psychological sciences (BPS, 1988) and is about to embark upon a study of the future of professional psychology. The BPS has produced a register of chartered psychologists which secures professional boundaries and provides more control over membership and psychological practice.

It is here that distinctions are drawn between professionals with psychology degrees (some of whom are apparently engaged in activities such as family work, stress management, counselling) and those with post-graduate qualifications in psychology who may become chartered psychologists.

It is too early to say what effect this will have on the often close, joint work between psychologists and social workers – but it does suggest separation – as the BPS chartered psychologist scheme was set up to distinguish between psychological practice and that of allied disciplines.

As we have argued, psychologists and social workers need to recognise common ground, issues of shared concern, and identify each other's strengths to mutual advantage. This is best done in areas of reseach (such as some of those discussed in this volume) and also in terms of academic input to social work training courses. *Psychologists* should teach psychology, which should be acknowledged as such. However, it also needs to be taught with a sympathetic and clear understanding of the context of practice.

References

Ainsworth, M.S. (1964) 'Patterns of attachment behaviour shown by the infant in interaction with his mother', *Merril-Palmer Quarterly*, 10, pp. 51–58.

Allport, G.W. (1937) *Personality*, London, Constable.

Allport, G.W. (1961) *Pattern and Growth in Personality*, London, Holt.

Argyle, M. (1978) *The Psychology of Interpersonal Behaviour*, 4th edn, London, Penguin.

Argyle, M. (1988) *Bodily Communication*, 2nd edn, London, Methuen.

Aronson, E. (1988) *The Social Animal*, 5th edn, New York, Freeman.

Badinter, E. (1980) *The Myth of Motherhood: An Historical View of the Maternal Instinct*, London, Souvenir Press.

Bandura, A. (1971) *Social Learning Theory*, New York, General Learning Press.

Barclay Report (1982) 'The role and tasks of social workers', London, NISW.

Bayne, R. (1980) 'Interpretations and uses of research on "Barnum" personality statements', *British Journal of Guidance and Counselling*, 8 (2), pp. 233–6.

Bayne, R. (1988) 'Psychological type as a model of personality development', *British Journal of Guidance and Counselling*, 16 (2), pp. 167–175.

Bayne, R. (1989) 'Four approaches to increasing self-awareness', in P. Herriot (ed.) *Handbook of Assessment in Organisations*, London, Wiley.

Benson, H. (1977) *The Relaxation Response*, London, Collins Fontana Paperbacks.

Bernard, J. (1976) *The Future of Marriage*, Harmondsworth, Penguin.

Berne, E. (1966) *Principles of Group Treatment*, New York, Oxford University Press.

Bion, W.R. (1961) *Experiences in Groups*, London, Tavistock.

Bloch, S. (1982) *What is Psychotherapy?*, Oxford, Oxford University Press.

Bond, M. (1986) *Stress and Self-awareness: A Guide for Nurses*, Oxford, Heinemann.

Bowlby, J. (1951) *Maternal Care and Mental Health*, Geneva, World Health Organisation; New York, Shocken Books.

Breakwell, G. (1989) *Facing Physical Violence*, London, BPS/Routledge.

Brenner, D. (1982) *The Effective Psychotherapist*, Oxford, Pergamon.

Bremner, J.G. (1988) *Infancy*, Oxford, Blackwell.
British Association for Counselling (BAC) (1985) *Code of Ethics and Practice*, Rugby, BAC.
'The future of the psychological sciences', (1988), BPS Report.
Broverman, I.K. (1970) 'Sex role stereotypes and clinical judgements of mental health', *Journal of Consulting Psychology*, 34, pp. 1–7.
Brown, A. (1979) *Groupwork*, London, Heinemann.
Burman, E. (ed.) (1989) *Feminists and Psychological Practice*, London, Sage.
Cartwright, D. and Zander, A. (1968) (eds) *Group Dynamics: Research and Theory*, New York, Harper and Row.
Castleman, M. (1988) *Making Love*, London, Penguin.
CCETSW Discussion Paper no. 2 (1967) 'Human growth and behaviour as a subject of study for social workers'.
CCETSW Paper 20, (9 February 1988) 'The qualifying diploma in social work'.
Clegg, F. (1988) 'Disasters: can psychologists help the survivors?', *The Psychologist*, vol. 1, 4, pp. 134–5.
Cohen, S. and Taylor, L. (1972) *Psychological Survival*, Harmondsworth, Penguin.
Cook, M. (1979) *Perceiving Others*, London, Methuen.
Costa, P.T. and McCrae, R.R. (1986) 'Personality stability and its implications for clinical psychology', *Clinical Psychology Review*, 6 (5), pp. 407–23.
Curtis Committee, (1946) *Report of the Care of Children Committee*, HMSO.
Dachowski, M.M. (1987) 'A convergence of the tender-minded and the tough-minded?', *American Psychologist*, 42, pp. 886–887.
Danbury, H. (1986) *Teaching Practical Social Work*, Aldershot, Gower.
Davies, G.M. (1988) 'The use of video in child abuse trials', *The Psychologist: Bulletin of the British Psychological Society*, 1, pp. 20–2.
Davies, W. (1988) 'How not to get hit', *The Psychologist*, May, pp. 175–6.
Dickson, A. (1987) *A Woman in Your Own Right*, London, Quartet Books.
Dinnerstein, D. (1976) *The Rocking of the Cradle and the Ruling of the World*, New York, Harper and Row.
Douglas, J.W.B. and Bloomfield, J.M. (1958) *Children Under Five*, London, Allen and Unwin.
Dryden, W. (1984) (ed.) *Individual Therapy in Britain*, London, Harper and Row.
Dominclli, L. (1988) *Anti-Racist Social Work*, London, Macmillan.
Douglas, T. (1978) *Basic Groupwork*, London, Tavistock.
Duck, S. (1983) *Friends, For Life*, Brighton, Harvester Press.
Duck, S. (1986) *Human Relationships*, London, Sage.
Eckerman, C.O. and Whatly, J.L. (1977) 'Toys and social interaction between infant peers', *Child Development*, 48, pp. 1645–56.
Egan, G. (1986) *The Skilled Helper*, 3rd edn, Monterey, Brooks/Cole.
Ekman, P. and Friesen, W.V. (1975) *Unmasking the Face*, London, Prentice-Hall.
Elliott, S. (1985) 'A rationale for psychosocial intervention in the prevention of postnatal depression', Paper presented at the Women in Psychology Conference, Cardiff.

Epstein, S. (1979) 'The stability of behaviour 1: On predicting most of the people much of the time', *Journal of Personality and Social Psychology*, 37, pp. 1097–1126.

Erikson, E.H. (1968) *Childhood and Society*, New York, Norton.

Evison, R. and Horobin, R. (1988) 'Co-counselling', in Rowan, J. and Dryden, W. (1988) (eds) *Innovative Therapy in Britain*, Milton Keynes, Open University.

Festinger, J.R.P. and Raven, B.H. (1959) *Social Pressures in Informal Groups: A Study of a Housing Community*, London, Harper and Row.

Finer Report (1974) *Report of the Committee on One-Parent Families*, HMSO.

Forgas, J.P. (1985) *Interpersonal Behaviour*, Oxford, Pergamon.

Freud, S. (1949) *An Outline of Psychoanalysis*, New York, Norton.

Freud, S. (1922) *Group Psychology and the Analysis of the Ego*, London, Hogarth.

French, J.R.P. and Raven, B.H. (1959) 'The bases of social power' in Cartwright, *Studies in Social Power*, Ann Arbor, Michigan, University of Michigan Press.

Funder, D.C. (1987) 'Errors and mistakes: evaluating the accuracy of social judgment', *Psychological Bulletin*, 101, pp. 75–90.

Gendlin, E.T. (1981) *Focusing*, 2nd edn, London, Bantam.

Gerber, I. *et al.* (1975) 'Brief therapy to the aged and bereaved' in B. Shoenberg *et al.* (eds), *Bereavement: Its Psychosocial aspects'*, New York, Columbia University Press.

Garfinkel, M. (1967) *Studies in Ethnomethodology*, Englewood, Cliffs, New Jersey, Prentice Hall.

Gilmore, S.K. (1973) *The Counselor-in-Training*, London, Prentice Hall.

Goffman, E. (1968) *Asylums*, Harmondsworth, Penguin.

Greenberg, L.S. and Dompierre, L.M. (1981) 'Specific effects of Gestalt two-chair dialogue on intrapsychic conflict in counselling', *Journal of Counseling Psychology*, 28 (4), pp. 288–94.

Greenberg, L.S. and Safran J.D. (1989) 'Emotion in psychotherapy', *American Psychologist*, 44 (1), pp. 19–29.

Gregory, R.L. (1977) *Eye and Brain*, 3rd edn, London, Weidenfeld and Nicolson.

Griffiths, R. (1988) *Community Care: Agenda for Action*, DHSS.

Herbert, M. (1981) *Psychology for Social Workers*, London, Macmillan.

Hargie, O. (1906) (ed.) *A Handbook of Communication Skills*, London, Croom Helm.

Harré, R. and Secord, P.F. (1972) *The Exploration of Social Behaviour*, Oxford, Blackwell.

Harvey, P. (1988) *Health Psychology*, London, Longman.

Hollway, W. (1989) *Subjectivity and Method in Psychology*, London, Sage.

Hopson, B. (1981a) 'Counselling and helping', in Griffiths, D., *Psychology and Medicine*, London, BPS and Macmillan.

Hopson, B. (1981b) 'Transition: understanding and managing personal change', in Griffiths, D., *Psychology and Medicine*, London, BPS and Macmillan.

Howe, D. (1987) *An Introduction to Social Work Theory*, Aldershot, Wildwood House.

Hudson, B.L. and Macdonald, G.M. (1986) *Behavioural Social Work: An Introduction*, London, Macmillan.

Hughes, M. *et al.* (1980) *Nurseries Now*, Harmondsworth, Penguin.

Horner, M.S. (1974) 'Towards an understanding of achievement–related conflicts in women', in J. Stacey and J. Daniels (eds) *And Jill Came Tumbling After: Sexism in American Education*, New York, Dell.

Inskipp, F. and Johns, H. (1983, and 1985) *Principles of Counselling: series I and II (for BBC radio; cassettes and notes from Alexia Publications, 2 Market Terrace, St Leonards-on-Sea, East Sussex).*

Inskipp, F. and Johns, H. (1984) 'Developmental eclecticism: Egan's skills model of helping', in Dryden, W. (ed.) Individual Therapy in Britain, London, Harper and Row.

Ivey, A.E., Ivey, M.B. and Simek-Downing, K. (1987) *Counselling and Psychotherapy: Integrating Skills, Theory, and Practice*, 2nd edn, London, Prentice-Hall.

Jaques, E. (1955) 'Social systems as a defence against persecutory and depressive anxiety' in M. Klein *et al.* (eds) *New directions in Psychoanalysis*, London, Tavistock.

Janis, I.L. (1972) *Victims of Groupthink: A Psychological Study of Foreign Policy Decision and Fiascos*, Boston, Houghton Mifflin.

Jones, M. (1968) *Social Psychiatry in Practice*, Harmondsworth, Penguin.

Kagan, N. (1984) 'Interpersonal process recall: basic methods and recent research', in D. Larsen (ed.) *Teaching Psychological Skills*, Monterey, California, Brooks/Cole.

Keirsey, D. and Bates, M. (1978) *Please Understand Me: Character and Temperament Types*, 3rd edn, Del Mar, California, Prometheus Nemesis Books.

Kenniston, K. (1977) *All Our Children: The American Family Under Pressure*, New York, Harcourt.

Kenrick, D.T. and Funder, D.C. (1988) 'Profiting from controversy: lessons from the person-situation debate', *American Psychologist*, 43 (1), pp. 23–34.

Kincey, V. (1974) 'The Evaluation of a bereavement counselling service', MSc Thesis, University of Manchester.

Klaus, H.M. and Kennell, J.M. (1976) *Maternal Infant Bonding*, St Louis, Missouri, Mosby.

Kitzinger, C. (1987) *The Social Construction of Lesbianism*, London, Sage.

Kohlberg, L. (1969) 'Stage and sequence: The cognitive-developmental approach to socialisation' in D.A. Goslin (ed.) *Handbook of Socialisation Theory and Research*, Chicago, Rand McNally.

Kohlberg, L. (1976) 'Moral stages and moralisation: the cognitive-developmental approach' in T. Lickona (ed.) *Moral Development and Behaviour*, New York, Holt, Rinehart and Winston.

Konopka, G. (1963) *Social Groupwork: A Helping Process*, Englewood Cliffs, New Jersey, Prentice-Hall.

La Fontaine, J. (1989) 'Child sexual abuse: an ESRC research briefing', in *After Abuse*, British Agencies for Adoption and Fostering.

Lee, P. and Pithers, D. (1980) 'Radical residential child care: Trojan horse or non-runner', in M. Brake and R. Bailey (eds) *Radical Social Work and Practice*, London, Arnold.

Leonard, P. (1984) *Personality and Ideology*, London, Macmillan.

Lewis, C. (1986) *Becoming a Father*, Milton Keynes, Open University Press.

Ley, P. (1988) *Communicating with Patients*, London, Croom Helm.

Lord, C.G., Lepper, M.R. and Preston, E. (1984) 'Considering the opposite: a corrective strategy for social judgment', *Journal of Personality and Social Psychology*, 47 (6), pp. 1231–43.

Maas, M. (1980) 'Research and Knowledge base', in *Discovery and Development in Social Work Education*, Vienna, International Association of Schools SW Publications.

Maguire, P. (1981) 'Doctor-patient skills', in M. Argyle (ed.) *Social Skills and Health*, London, Methuen.

Martin, D. (1962) *Adventure in Psychiatry*, London, Cassirer.

Matarazzo, R. and Patterson, D. (1986) 'Methods of teaching therapeutic skill', in S. Garfield and A. Bergin (eds) *Handbook of Psychotherapy and Behaviour Change*, Chichester, Wiley.

Mearns, D. and Thorne, B. (1988) *Person-Centred Counselling in Action*, London, Sage.

Menzies, I.E.P. (1970) *The Functioning of Social Systems as a Defence against Anxiety*, London, Tavistock Institute of Human Relations.

Milgram, S. (1974) *Obedience to Authority*, New York, Harper and Row.

Miller, E.J. and Gwynne, G.V. (1972) *A Life Apart*, London, Tavistock.

Mills, C.K. and Wooster, A.D. (1987) 'Crying in the counselling situation', *British Journal of Guidance and Counselling*, 15 (2), pp. 125–30.

Mitchell, J. (1974) *Psychoanalysis and Feminism*, Harmondsworth, Pelican.

Monckton Inquiry (1945) HMSO.

Moreno, J.L. (1934) *Who shall Survive? A New Approach to the Problems of Human Interrelations*, Washington D.C., Nervous and Mental Diseases Publishing Co.

Mueller, E. and Brenner, J. (1977) 'The origin of social skills and interaction among playgroup toddlers', *Child Development*, 48, pp. 854–61.

Munro, E.A., Manthei, R.J. and Small, J.J. (1983) *Counselling*, rev. edn, Auckland, Methuen.

Murgatroyd, S. (1985) *Counselling and Helping*,. London, BPS/Methuen.

Murgatroyd, S. and Woolfe, R. (1982) *Coping with Crisis*, London, Harper and Row.

Murray-Parkes, C. (1972) *Bereavement: Studies of Grief in Adult Life*, London, Tavistock.

Myers, I.B. (1980) *Gifts Differing*, Palo Alto, California, Consulting Psychologists Press.

Myers, I.B. and McCaulley, M. (1985) *Manual: A Guide to the Development and Use of the Myers-Briggs Type Indicator*, Palo Alto, California, Consulting Psychologists Press.

Nelson-Jones, R. (1988) *Practical Counselling and Helping Skills*, 2nd edn, London, Cassell.

Newson, J. and Newson, E. (1976) *Seven Years Old in the Home Environment*, London, George Allen and Unwin.

170 *References*

Nichols, K.A. (1984) *Psychological Care in Physical Illness*, Beckenham, Croom Helm.

Nichols, K.A. (1988) 'Practising what we preach', *The Psychologist*, February, pp. 50–1.

Nicholson, J. (1984) *Men and Women*, Oxford, Oxford University Press.

Nicolson, P. and Bayne, R. (1984) *Applied Psychology for Social Workers*, London, Macmillan.

Nicolson, P. (1988) 'The social psychology of "post-natal depression"', unpublished Phd Thesis, University of London.

Norman, D.A. (1982) *Learning and Memory*, London, Freeman.

Older, J. (1977) 'Four taboos that may limit the success of psychotherapy', *Psychiatry*, 40, pp. 197–204.

Packman, J. (1975) *The Child's Generation*, London, Blackwell and Robertson.

Parke, R.D. *et al.* (1979) *Child Psychology: A Contemporary Viewpoint*, New York, McGraw-Hill.

Patterson, C.H. (1984) 'Empathy, warmth and genuineness: a review of reviews', *Psychotherapy* 21 (4), pp. 431–8.

Payne, M. (1982) *Working in Teams*, London, Macmillan.

Piaget, J. (1932) *The Moral Judgement of the Child*, New York, Free Press.

Pincus, L. (1976) *Death and the Family*, London, Faber and Faber.

Polak, P.R. *et al.* (1973) 'Crisis intervention in acute bereavement', Colorado, draft paper from Fort Logan Community Health Centre.

Progoff, I. (1975) *At a Journal Workshop*, New York, Dialogue House.

Rainer, T. (1980) *The New Diary*, London, Angus and Robertson.

Raphael, B. (1977) 'Preventative intervention with the recently bereaved', *Archives of General Psychology*, 34, pp. 1450–4.

Reddy, M. (1987) *The Manager's Guide to Counselling at Work*, London, BPS/Methuen.

Richards, M. and Righton, P. (1972) *Social Work Education in Conflict*, London, NISW Papers.

Richards, M. and Light, P. (1986) *Children of Social Worlds*, Polity Press, Cambridge.

Richardson, D. (1981) 'Sexism in Social Work', *Community Care*, November.

Richardson, J. (1987) 'Cognition, memory and the menstrual cycle', paper presented at the BPS London Conference.

Richman, N. (1976) 'Depression in mothers of pre-school children', *Journal of Child Psychology and Psychiatry*, 17, pp. 25–78.

Rogers, C. (1961) *On Becoming a Person*, Boston, Houghton Mifflin.

Rogers, C. (1975) 'Empathic: an unappreciated way of being', reprinted in Rogers, C. (1980) *A Way of Being*, Boston, Houghton Mifflin.

Rogers, C. (1978) *Carl Rogers on Personal Power*, London, Constable.

Rogers, C. (1987) 'Comments on the issue of equality in psychotherapy', *Journal of Humanistic Psychology*, 27 (1), pp. 38–40.

Rowan, J. (1983) *The Reality Game: A Guide to Humanistic Counselling and Therapy*, London, Routledge.

Rowan, J. (1988) 'Counselling and the psychology of furniture', *Counselling*, 64, pp. 21–4.

Rutter, M. (1972) *Maternal Deprivation Re-assessed*, Harmondsworth, Penguin.

Rutter, M. (1989) 'Pathways from childhood to adult life', *Journal of Child Psychology and Psychiatry*, 30 (1), pp. 23–51.

Sayers, J. (1982) *Biological Politics*, London, Tavistock.

Scheflen, A.C. (1964) 'The Significance of posture in communication systems,' *Psychiatry*, 27, pp. 316–31.

Seebohm Report (1968) *Report of the Committee on Local Authority and Allied Personal Social Services*, HMSO.

Smail, D. (1987) *Taking Care*, London, Dent.

Smith, C.R. (1982) *Social Work with the Dying and Bereaved*, London, Macmillan.

Smith, H.C. (1973) *Sensitivity Training: The Scientific Understanding of Individuals*, London, McGraw-Hill.

Sommer, B. (1987) 'Cognition and the menstrual cycle: a survey', paper presented at the BPS London Conference.

Spitz, R.A. (1945) 'Hospitalisation: an inquiry into the genesis of psychiatric conditions in early childhood', *Psychoanalytic Studies of the Child*, 1, pp. 53–74.

Stevens, A. (1989) 'The politics of caring', *The Psychologist*, 2, (3), pp. 110–10.

Stewart, V. (1987) *The MBTI Practitioner's Guide*, Bristol, Myers-Briggs Users Group (UK).

Stiles, W.B., Shapiro, D.A. and Elliott, R. (1986) 'Are all psychotherapies equivalent?', *American Psychologist*, 41, pp. 165–80.

Storr, A. (1979) *The Art of Psychotherapy*, London, Secker and Warburg/Heinemann.

Sutton, C. (1987) 'Social workers as applied psychologists: a plea for sensitive support', *Bulletin of the BPS*, 34, pp. 465–7.

Tallent, N. (1983) *Psychological Report Writing*, 2nd edn, London, Prentice-Hall.

Tavris, C. and Wade, C. (1984) *The Longest War*, 2nd edn, London, Harcourt.

Tizard, B. (1975) *Adoption: A Second Chance*, London, Open Books.

Tuckman, B.W. (1965) 'Developmental sequence in small groups', *Psychological Bulletin*, 63, no. 6, pp. 384–99.

Twelvetrees, A. (1982) *Community Work*, London, Macmillan.

Ussher, J.M. (1989) *The Psychology of the Female Body*, London, Routledge.

Vetere, A. and Gale, A. (1987) *Ecological Studies of Family Life*, Chichester, Wiley.

Walker, D. (1985) 'Writing and reflection' in Boud, D., Keogh, R. and Walker, D., *Reflection: Turning Experience into Learning*, London, Kogan Page.

Waxer, P.H. (1978) *Non-verbal Aspects of Psychotherapy*, London, Praeger.

Wilkinson, S. (ed.) (1986) *Feminist Social Psychology*, Milton Keynes, Open University Press.

Williams, J.H. (1974) *Psychology of Women: Behaviour in a Biosocial Context*, New York, Norton.

Woollett, E.A. (1987) 'Why motherhood is popular: an analysis of accounts of mothers and childless women', paper presented at the Women in Psychology Conference. Brunel.

Zilbergeld, B. (1983) *The Shrinking of America: Myths of Psychological Change*, Boston, Little.

Zimbardo, P.G. *et al.* (1976) *Influencing Attitudes and Changing Behaviour*, 2nd edn, London, Addison-Wesley.

Index